INGRID CONLIFFE-EASTON

COME OUT
OF THE
Rain
YOU'VE GOT THIS!

COME OUT OF THE RAIN
You've Got This

Ingrid Conliffe-Easton
ingridconliffe@gmail.com

ISBN: 978-1-949826-25-8
Printed in the USA.
All rights reserved

Published by: EAGLES GLOBAL BOOKS | Frisco, Texas
Cover & interior designed by DestinedToPublish.com | (773) 783-2981

Acknowledgments

This book is dedicated to my dearly departed mother, who loved and spoiled her "baby" to a fault. My loving husband Richard, my greatest supporter and friend; my dear and precious children, Montra (my princess), Fabian (my mini me), and Richard-Harvey (I dare not put in print my endearing name for him). They have been with me every step of the way, and they seem to think I can do and achieve anything. These children have also taught me the challenges of parenthood, because they are all different, but I think I am a better person for it.

Then along came Meliyah, my first and only granddaughter at this time, who also believes there is nothing her grandma cannot do and loves to say, "Grandma, God tells you everything." To my brother Leslie and sister Colleen, who I absolutely love and who have contributed greatly to my upbringing. Being the youngest sibling indeed has its benefits to this day.

To my wonderful niece Nandi, who I know wanted to assist in reading my manuscript, but life got in the way. Nevertheless, her words of encouragement were appreciated. To my dear and special friend Kyekyenika Terrell, who came over and read my manuscript and was a great encourager throughout the process.

To all of you, I want to say publicly that I love you unconditionally. Thank you all for being a part of my life and this journey.

Contents

COME OUT OF THE RAIN — YOU'VE GOT THIS

Introduction

Over the past 10 years or so, I have been receiving countless prophecies about God wanting me to write a book. I would go to conferences and be asked, "When are you going to write the book? What about the book?" I had no idea what I should write on and had not even begun to have a title for a book. As time passed – actually years – one day I received a prophecy and a phrase was used. Immediately the Holy Spirit said, "That's the title for your book."

One would think that I was now charged and eager to begin writing, but that was not so. Again, some time passed, and one day I awoke and clearly heard another phrase that was to be an addition to the title of the book. Would you believe that again I procrastinated? Now my battle was, how can I turn this title into a book?

> *"The plans of the heart belong to man, but the answer of the tongue is from the Lord." Proverbs 16:1 (ESV)*

> *"I know that You can do all things, and that no purpose of Yours can be thwarted." Job 42:2 (NASB)*

Then, hallelujah! I was introduced to the EITI (Eagles International Training Institute) authorship course. I became excited for a brief moment, but then the mental struggles started all over again. I am sure that many of you can identify with my struggles. How many times the Lord speaks to us, and yet we find ourselves battling to do what He asks. I had the title, but again, what would the book be about? After much going back and forth in my head, I was able to formulate an outline for what I wanted to address. It was a battle but I can identify with the scripture:

> *"Many plans are in a man's heart, but the counsel of the Lord will stand" (Proverbs 19:21, NASB).*

> *"Being confident of this very thing, that he which hath begun a good work in you will perform it until the day of Jesus Christ." Philippians 1:6 (KJV)*

The truth is, this book came to life after I asked the Father for advice. Often, we attempt things using our own strengths and abilities. That would have been easy, because I am blessed with many abilities, but I wanted to be directed by God about the path I should take.

I trust that as you read this book, your lives will be encouraged, challenged, and changed. I am not oblivious to the fact that you might have heard or read similar messages before, but I encourage you to you allow the Holy Spirit to breathe a fresh wind as you read. That the word of God never gets old; it is like fresh dew.

"Let my teaching fall like rain and my words descend like dew, like showers on new grass, like abundant rain on tender plants."
Deuteronomy 32:2 (NIV)

COME OUT OF THE RAIN — YOU'VE GOT THIS

Chapter 1
Come Out of the Rain

In writing this narrative, I want my readers to be gripped with what God's love and faithfulness can produce in a life given over to Him. The scripture says:

> *"But as it is written, Eye hath not seen, nor ear heard, neither have entered into the heart of man, the things which God hath prepared for them that love him." 1 Corinthians 2:9 (KJV)*

My life is one that was not born into affluence but a life that came out on the other side in triumph and success, all because of the grace of God. I pause to say,

> *"Faithful is he that calleth you, who also will do it" (1 Thessalonians 5:24, KJV).*

As I look over my life, I think of the many times I literally had to come out of the "rain." However, this book, though written about my own life, also encompasses the people and situations I have encountered during my journey. There are many I have identified with, counseled, and empathized with over the years. From a humble beginning to where I am now, I can honestly say without it being a cliché, *"Look what the Lord has done."*

Many of us mistakenly equate this saying with our earthly possessions, but for me, it also represents the person and the new creation I am in Christ. There is a saying that is embraced by many: "It's not where or how you started but how you finish."

For the Christian, however, the outcome is predetermined if we allow God to reign and rule in our lives, because with Him we win. He is always by our sides, ready to guide and protect us.

The battles we face, the obstacles we encounter, the disappointments we experience, can never void the power of God's promises to us. The Bible is full of God's promises and reminds us constantly that He is faithful.

> *"The Lord is good to all; he has compassion on all he has made." Psalm 145:9 (NIV)*

There is a plethora of scriptures that remind us that our heavenly Father is always there by our sides. Even though we mistakenly pray, "Father (or Lord) be with us today," He really can't answer this prayer because He has already said, "I will never leave you nor forsake you."

> *"... Do not be afraid or terrified because of them, for the LORD your God goes with you; he will never leave you nor forsake you." Deuteronomy 31:6 (NIV)*

> *"No one will be able to stand against you all the days of your life. As I was with Moses, so I will be with you; I will never leave you nor forsake you." Joshua 1:5 (NIV)*

Although this is a promise made to Joshua, it belongs to every believer, for our God will not abandon His people into the hands of the enemy, and neither would He leave us in times of distress. **He's got you, so you've got this.**

Whatever your "this" is, in your life currently, even in this season, at this time, in this moment – whether it be anger, depression, emotional problems, fear, finances, health, loneliness, marital problems, rejection, rebellion, and the list can go on – **know that God's got you.**

As we journey together through this book, traversing the ups and downs, the negatives and the positives of life, the overall picture I want you to grasp is: The unfailing love of the Lord never ceases!

> *"...By his mercies we have been kept from complete destruction." Lamentations 3:22 (NTL)*

The God of the universe is faithful in all that He does. It behooves us to trust and depend on Him. Together, as we are encouraged to come out of the "rain," I want you to look back over your life. Take an inventory, identify the things you have been through, the hardships you have faced, and realize that you came through them all because God had always got you. He said:

> *"And teaching them to obey everything I have commanded you. And surely, I am with you always, to the very end of the age." Matthew 28:20 (NIV)*

Unfortunately, if we have been involved in Christendom for any period of time, we begin to accept things and situations that are contrary to the word of God, because we allow them to become norms in our lives. Take sickness, for instance: after diagnosis, many tend to identify with the sickness, whatever it is. For example, we say things like "my diabetes," "my arthritis," "my terrible headache," etc. Some of these situations cause us to buckle under them, and at times, it seems as if there is no way out, and our faith starts to wane.

> *"Do not conform to the pattern of this world, but be transformed by the renewing of your mind. Then you will be able to test and approve what God's will is—his good, pleasing and perfect will." Romans 12:2 (NIV)*

The reason for this is that we easily accept the enemy's attacks and disruption of our lives as badges of honor, thinking and believing that these things make us holy. The Bible speaks of the apostle Paul: *"I will show him how much he must suffer for my name" (Acts 9:16, NIV)*. We tend to make Paul's suffering our example, but this situation is not a blanket statement meant for all Christians.

The irony is, we also quote myths and old wives' fables as though they are scriptures and start believing them. We don't set out to build our faith on myths, but because they are passed down from one generation to the next, they tend to shape the way many of us think. For example, take the saying "God helps those who help themselves" – the premise itself is not wrong, but it is not a scripture verse. Scripture admonishes us to:

> *"Have nothing to do with godless myths and old*

*wives' tales; rather, train yourself to be godly." 1
Timothy 4:7 (NIV)*

The intent here is to allow us to understand and perhaps remind us that we are handpicked:

*"But [in spite of all your doubts] you are a
chosen people, a royal priesthood, a holy nation,
God's special possession, that you may declare
the praises of him who called you out of darkness
into his wonderful light." 1 Peter 2:9 (NIV)*

One recurring theme throughout this book is the fact that, ultimately, we are all responsible for our own actions and lives. Therefore, as you traverse through the pages of this book, my prayer is that you would embark on a journey that is relatable to you in some way; that you would find hope, love, acceptance, and forgiveness; and that you would be enthused with, and appreciative of, the love and grace of God.

Chapter 2

Welcome to my Journey

Moments of My Childhood

Children are a gift from the Lord; they are a reward from him. Psalm 127:3 (NLT)

Childhood is the period of one's life when one is innocent and most vulnerable. A time when childhood memories are formed and when the behaviors of others can leave deep impressions. Although childhood memories can be sparse and far between, many believe they are never really lost. Instead, they somehow seem to find a way to become embedded deep within the recesses of the mind. Childhood gives us our first view of the world and helps form our perspectives. Yes, those views can be misconstrued, because the ability to psychoanalyze them is not yet formed. However, many can attest to having flashbacks of moments, events, and things from childhood.

I can remember many things about my childhood in Guyana to this day, which are pleasant overall. My mother was a single parent with three children; she found herself in this position because she came from a humble beginning and was taken advantage of, and notably, she walked in that throughout her entire life. She worked as a maid and was loved by her employers. I recall going with my sister to the house where she worked on Saturday – I looked forward to that time because her employers were cordial and made us feel comfortable.

One thing that stood out to me during that time was that anything my mom learned in that house, she taught us at home. I was very young, my mom taught me to set the dining table, which became my responsibility at Christmas time. Many of us can attest that Christmas time is when folks bring out all the fine china. To this day, I can set a dining table with all the required dishes and cutlery on it.

> *"Train up a child in the way he should go: and when he is old, he will not depart from it."* Proverbs 22:6 (KJV)

As a parent, she could not afford all of the niceties of life, but she did her best to make sure that my siblings and I had a sense of normalcy. She took my sister and me everywhere she went (my brother was much older). Although there were times when we were just getting by, my mom had a sense of pride. When she took us to visit friends and family, we seldom would accept or eat anything they offered because we were always "full" or had just eaten. One reason for this was that she just didn't like eating anything from other people if she hadn't seen how it was prepared, but another reason, I soon realized, was that she did not want to be indebted to anyone. We did not have much, but we were never hungry.

> *"He has filled the hungry with good things, and the rich he has sent away empty." Luke 1:53 (ESV)*

Clothing was another matter. On particular Saturdays, there would be a flea market in a school building across from the public market. This is where my mother would purchase secondhand clothes for me, because that was what she could afford at that time. I can remember sometimes going there with her. No one really knew where I got my clothes, because I picked out the things I wanted – most of which were shorts, pants, and tops, being the "tomboy" that I was – and wore them confidently. The thing is, though, I can recall looking around when we were exiting that building, to make sure no one I knew saw me coming out of there.

"Strength and dignity are her clothing, and she smiles at the future." Proverbs 31:25 (NASB)

There were also the good times, like when my mom would go to the market. She would leave the house at about 5 a.m. on Saturday mornings, while we were still asleep, to go and buy our weekly produce. She would tell us that by going that early, she would be ahead of the weekend crowd and so could be back early.

She would return balancing a basket on her head with the things she had purchased. When mangos were in season, it was a joy; we would sit on the floor around a large bowl of water eating "touch" mangos – that is, mangos that were bruised, not the best of the bunch, but tasted good anyway. Those were fun times.

"Let them give thanks to the Lord for his unfailing love and his wonderful deeds for mankind, for he satisfies the thirsty and fills the hungry with good things." Psalm 107:8-9 (NIV)

Then there were the times when we were taken advantage of. I was made aware from a young age of the disadvantages that single mothers face when there is no male, or what is commonly called a father figure, in the household. My mom was a very docile individual, never confrontational. She never seemed to have the wherewithal to defend herself: the complete opposite of her confrontational last child.

We were taken advantage of on many levels. My mother had one brother who lived way outside the city limits, in what we referred to as the "countryside," and although he had twelve children, they were all far away. We visited occasionally, but in the city, we were basically alone. At one time, we lived in a two-family apartment and were constantly being harassed and abused by the family living in front of us.

> *"For he will command his angels concerning you to guard you in all your ways." Psalm 91:11 (NIV)*

They really took advantage of us. I remember one day when my mom and I had to hide under the bed. We were in the bedroom, and my sister and a young woman my mom had taken in to live with us were in the kitchen across the hall.

My mom and I heard a commotion and looked out the bedroom window, and we saw a group of family members from the neighbors in the front of us. They were being loud, and we had no idea what was happening.

Unfortunately for us, one of them saw us. The individual

shouted, "They're in the bedroom!" We tried to get to the kitchen that was built like a fortress, but we could not make, so we hid under the bed.

That was one of the most terrifying days of my young life. We had no idea if they were going to jump over the bedroom walls (which did not reach the ceiling), as one of them shouted, "They're under the bed!" Thankfully, no one came over the wall. We remained under the bed for a long time after the family left before venturing out. To this day, I have no idea what their intentions were, but what I know is that the Lord did protect us that day.

"Believe in the Lord Jesus, and you will be saved – you and your household." Acts 16:31 (NIV)

At some point, my mom decided she wanted her own house, so she joined a self-help group that allowed people to come together and build their own houses as a community. The place where the meetings were held was a far distance from where we lived. We had no means of transportation, so we had to walk back and forth. We were always so tired because it was a school night and the meetings were long.

On our way back home, my sister and I would be on either side of my mother, sleeping as we walked. I don't know how she did it, but she was committed. She walked with us hanging on the side of her week after week, month after month. What I learned later was that she had no guarantee that her name was going to be drawn, but she persevered.

"We want each of you to show this same

diligence to the very end, so that what you hope for may be fully realized." Hebrews 6:11 (NIV)

Eventually, she was told that she was chosen to be a part of the community to receive a house. The word "self-help" meant exactly what you think it means. There were about twenty-five families chosen to get a plot of land. We all worked together clearing the large area of land donated by the government. It was back-breaking work, but each member of every family pitched in, regardless of age. I learned to make concrete blocks from a young age, among other things.

"Commit your work to the Lord, and your plans will be established." Proverbs 16:3 (ESV)

Finally, all the houses were built and each family got their house. It was a time of jubilation. But as fate would have it, our house was on a lot next to a large family. It seemed as if history was repeating itself. These folks were nosy, loud, and boisterous.

Even though we were folks who did not have much, they were engrossed in what was happening over at our house because of the way we conducted ourselves and the way we lived. They even encroached on our land by building their fence on a part of our property, and my mother could not or did not do anything about it.

"For God has not given us a spirit of timidity [or cowardice or fear] but of power and love and discipline." 2 Timothy 1:7 (NASB)

My sister was a beauty to behold in her younger years. It is not that she is no longer beautiful, but back then she was like the belle of the ball. They could not get enough of her. She was working, dressed beautifully, and bought herself a bicycle; she became the envy of most. The neighbor's children would use derogatory words whenever they saw her. Partly, I believe, because she was standoffish in her own way, unlike me, who was referred to as being a tomboy: I dressed like one, acted like one, and spoke like one. In my younger years, I had a real raspy-sounding voice. I walked on my toes with a bounce, and was ready to engage anyone and everything.

> *"Do not seek revenge or bear a grudge against anyone among your people, but love your neighbor as yourself. I am the Lord." Leviticus 19:18 (NIV)*

Looking back, I can see how my mother's acquiescence to most situations contributed to me being a bully. I exhibited every type of bullying there was back then – verbal, physical, and psychological. I made sure that no one could take advantage of me. I was so tough that "tomboy" and "bully" were synonymous when referring to me. No one messed with me; I was the leader of the pack.

Going home from school, I always had a group with me, some of them carrying my books (no backpacks back then). My own sister would not acknowledge me on the street because I was always in a fight.

It was like that until the day my mother's encounter with Jesus changed the course of my young life. I got home from school one afternoon and found my mom in tears. She had been listening to a preacher on the radio, Michael Patterson, for some time. She told me she had just seen a vision of Jesus and must find the preacher's church. So, one day, we set out to find this church, which was several miles away. She started attending regularly, and at some point, after that, my mom became a Christian.

"You will seek me and find me, when you seek me with all your heart." Jeremiah 29:13 (ESV)

I continued attending church with my mom. One summer night during service, a prophecy came forth. God called me daughter and told me what He would do with my life if I chose to serve Him. Wow! I was so excited that He called me daughter. Now I would have a Father – not that I did not know my father, but this was different. That night, when I was 12 years old, I became a Christian, and my life has never been the same.

"Love the Lord your God and keep his requirements, his decrees, his laws and his commands always." Deuteronomy 11:1 (NIV)

The scripture verse referenced at the beginning of this chapter (Psalm 127:3) should cause each of us to stop and think, for regardless of how we got here, we are gifts from God. Some of us might not have been born from the best of situations or circumstances – rape, incest, a single parent, or even unwanted by an otherwise loving couple. Nevertheless, no matter the path that got us here, God loves each and every one of us and had plans for us even before we were born. The scriptures cannot lie: they are yea and amen to all who believe. Knowing that God knows our end from the beginning is liberating in and of itself. The very thought causes my heart to leap with excitement – I trust yours does too.

"For you created my inmost being; you knit me together in my mother's womb. I praise you because I am fearfully and wonderfully made; your works are wonderful I know that full well. My frame was not hidden from you when I was made in the secret place, when I was woven together in the depths of the earth. Your eyes saw my unformed body; all the days ordained for me were written in your book before one of them came to be." Psalm 139:13-16 (NIV)

And He also said to Jeremiah: "Before I formed thee in the womb, I knew you; before you were born, I set you apart..." Jeremiah 1:5 (NIV)

Now, as part of God's family, I became acutely aware of my surroundings and the goings on around me. The interesting thing about life is, if we take time to reflect every so often, it can teach us many lessons. I would visit my friends and observe the dynamics in their home. I began to grasp the fact that having a dad in the home did not necessarily mean everything was dandy. You have probably come to that same realization too.

It begs the question, therefore, what makes a house a home? When we think about "home," it has a noticeably deeper meaning than "house," and this difference can evade our understanding. Remodeling shows such as Flip This House show us beautifully renovated houses; however, what should pique our interest is the point when these houses really become a home.

Naturally the house is breathtaking and gorgeous when finished, and its value is now thousands of dollars more;

but when does the house with all its affluence and beautifully decorated decor become a home?

Look around our towns, cities, counties and listen to the news: we are constantly bombarded with so many people living in gorgeous houses who kill and defraud each other for gain.

Doesn't that tell us that without true love, commitment, concern, and care for each other's wellbeing, a house can never really become a home? It is plain and simple: a house is a building and a structure.

> *"For every house is built by someone, but God is the builder of everything." Hebrews 3:4 (NIV)*

Therefore, when we think of a home, it should be a place much more becoming, made up of loving and caring individuals, where laughter, happiness, jokes, and fun abound. A home is that place, that safe place where people can relax and be themselves. It is a comfortable, convenient, cozy, and alluring sanctuary from outside influences and the world at large.

So, you see it takes a loving, caring, and committed family to make a house a home. And in spite of the hardships we faced, that was the home we had, and more so with the addition of my niece Nandi. She was a bundle of joy and became the center of our lives. We enjoyed ourselves even without a father figure.

> *"My people will live in peaceful dwelling places, in secure homes, in undisturbed places of rest." Isaiah 32:18 (NIV)*

Lack of a father figure never really mattered to me. We had a loving home, and I was certain of one thing above all else - my family and my heavenly Father loved me. So, my encouragement to you is, don't be dismayed and lose heart, for God's love is bountiful and free to all.

> *"See how great a love the Father has bestowed on us, that we would be called children of God..." 1 John 3:1 (NASB)*

> *"But as many as received Him, to them He gave the right to become children of God, even to those who believe in His name." John 1:12 (NASB)*

Therefore, regardless of how our childhood years were, we can take comfort in the fact that we made it through and we are here. Roller coaster or not, here we are, with different memories of our formative years, yet with the chance to change the trajectory of our family's lives moving forward. We now have a voice in how our own families look. The choices we make today are ours and ours alone.

So, whatever we did not like growing up, we can make sure it is not repeated.

> *"The reward of humility and the fear of the Lord are riches, honor, and life." Proverbs 22:4 (NIV)*

As you look at your life now, reflecting on your childhood, are your memories worth reliving or revisiting? Perhaps for many the answer might be no, but then the question becomes, have you buried the disappointments, rejections, and hurts associated with your upbringing? Remember that things buried can be resurrected. So, let us get rid of them forever, realizing today that all is not lost, because there is hope. The years may have gone by, but if our recollections still haunt us, we are encouraged to fear not. The God above is able to restore us to His original plan; for He is the Restorer of all things.

> *"'But I will restore you to health and heal your wounds,' declares the Lord...." Jeremiah 30:17 (NIV)*

> *"Instead of your shame you will receive a double portion, and instead of disgrace you will rejoice in your inheritance. And so, you will inherit a double portion in your land, and everlasting joy will be yours." Isaiah 61:7 (NIV)*

> *"'For I know the plans I have for you,' declares the Lord, 'plans to prosper you and not to harm you, plans to give you a hope and a future.'" Jeremiah 29:11 (NIV)*

Many years ago, Morris Chapman wrote a song titled "I Will Restore." Part of the lyrics are "I will restore, I will restore, I will restore to you all of **this** and more." Can I again ask you, what is your **this**? realizing that the Heavenly Father promises to restore.

The Bible is filled with hope when all else fails and seems to contradict that hope. Throughout the scriptures, restoration is a constant theme. God has always been willing and ready to restore us and make us whole again.

Be encouraged as you read these scriptures, and know that you, like me, are not a mistake. The Father above knew about you even before that seed was planted. He created you. Know that He's got you. In spite of everything, to Him you are uniquely you. No one else is like you.

Have you ever thought about the fact that there are billions of people on this earth and no two persons have the same fingerprints? How remarkable is that! This God who wants to be our Father has even numbered the hairs on our heads.

> *"Indeed, the very hairs on your head are all numbered. Don't be afraid; you are worth more than many sparrows." Luke 12:7 (NIV)*

> *"But there shall not a hair of your head perish." Luke 21:18 (KJV)*

We can surely rejoice in Him for His commitment to us and to mankind. Hallelujah! Our childhood hurts or disappointments do not define us today.

High School Reflections

> *"Do not be conformed to this world, but be transformed by the renewal of your mind, that by testing you may discern what is the will of God, what is good and acceptable, and perfect." Romans 12:2 (ESV)*

For some of us, high school represents the time in our lives when we began to assert ourselves. So, whether those days were good or bad, we can never seem to forget them.

This period of our lives left an indelible mark on us. They were the times when we tried to proclaim our independence, tried our utmost to fit in, tried to hang with the popular crowd, or perhaps had our first love relationship.

It was the period when our hormones were all over the place and our decisions changed from one day to the next. Many might be able to attest to the fact that high school represents some of the best or the worst days of our lives.

Looking back, many of us still reminisce on those high school days. For some of us, it gives us a euphoric sense of nostalgia because we did thrive during that period, while for others of us, high school represents the most hurtful and stressful four years of our young lives. Wherever we fall on this spectrum, one thing is for certain: if we are here, we all came through. It might not have been the way we wanted, but we are here to at least talk about it, even if it feels repulsive to do so.

"God is our refuge and strength, always ready to help in times of trouble." Psalm 46:1 (NLT)

As for me, my high school days were great. I remember entering high school wondering and being concerned about how I was going to fare as a new Christian.

Like my time in primary school, I was relatively popular, but adolescence was a confusing time as I sought to navigate my newfound Christian life. Things had to be different.

I had a great teacher, Mr. Randolph Scott, who saw my potential and would not allow me to get away with anything. I had this ability to remember something once I understood it when it was taught – some said I had a photographic memory.

So, I had the tendency to relax and cruise along without putting forth too much effort. I had just one rule: I must always finish as one of the top five in the class, and once that was accomplished, I was okay. Mr. Scott, though, would always be on my case, reminding me of my great potential and my ability to grasp concepts and things. He brought the best out of me.

> *"Walk with the wise and become wise, for a companion of fools suffers harm." Proverbs 13:20 (NIV)*

I had a very good girlfriend, Sandra; we got into trouble together and remain friends to this day. Then there was my very handsome male friend, Michael; we were very close. We were in primary school together and were both athletes. As a matter of fact, he won an athletic scholarship to a different high school and became the national champion in the 100- and 400-meter races. Everyone assumed we were in a relationship, even his brother, because we were so close.

I was the envy of the girls at his high school; they would send angry looks my way whenever they saw me. Once at a national meet, I fell after crossing the finish line, and in front of thousands of athletes and spectators, he came out, picked me up, and walked me around the field, hugging me. After that, even my teacher Mr. Scott asked me if we were both sure we were not in a relationship.

The sports I was involved in were very important to me

during high school. It was the period when I wanted to refine my craft. From a young age, I had won many awards – I was a very good sprinter and high jumper and was deemed a natural. But coaches would be upset with me about not having a training regimen, especially for high jumping. All my years as a high jumper in competitions, I would always finish in the top two. The coaches could not understand why I would not take that sport seriously.

Fear Impeded My Success.

No one ever suspected why I would not pursue high jumping intently, but I had a secret: the fact of the matter was I was very afraid. Many would remember that in the 60s and 70s there were two forms of high jumping – the scissors and the back flip. I could and would only do the scissors jump.

Some of the other competitors, on the other hand, could do the back flip. I controlled everything around me, and with the back flip I could not see the landing. Everyone kept saying I needed to learn the back flip if I wanted to jump higher, but I was so afraid, and that was why I eventually stopped high jumping.

I personally know what fear can do to someone. That is why I have such an aversion to seeing people being controlled by that evil spirit called fear. The Bible says that fear brings torment, and this is so true. When looking at the back flip, I saw all that could go wrong – a broken neck or a broken back, etc. Now, during high school, the back flip (if that is what it is still called) seemed to be the order of the day.

"For I am the Lord your God who takes hold of your right hand and says to you, do not fear; I will help you." Isaiah 41:13 (NIV)

"The Lord himself goes before you and will be with you; he will never leave you nor forsake you. Do not be afraid; do not be discouraged." Deuteronomy 31:8 (NIV)

I also played volleyball and ping-pong. I had a teacher, Mr. Donald Sinclair ("Flat-Tops," as we called him because of his hairstyle), who had a great influence on my life. Whenever he was on the volleyball court, I was sure to be a part of the game, which made some of my friends angry.

Ping-pong (table tennis) was also one of my passions, and the national table tennis champion Carol Davidson and I were really intimidating. We would usurp most of the time on the tennis table. The other kids were afraid of us; I guess we were acting a little like bullies.

I loved ping-pong so much that when I could not play in the tennis room, I would draw a table on the concrete floor in the classroom to play. By doing that, I developed a powerful back hand and slice stroke because the ball would bounce up high on the concrete.

I recall one semester, one of my girlfriends scored higher than I did in the finals, and she laughed at me. I was so upset that I told her in no uncertain terms, "From now on, you will never smell me." This was because of my unspoken rule that I had to be the brightest in my circle. Coupled with that, I had asked my mom to buy me a better ping-pong racquet following semester, and she had told me she could not afford it. So, gradually I let ping-pong go.

My involvement in athletics was so focused now that one could only imagine how distraught I was when, after eventually becoming a part of a leading athletic club (Southerners Athletic Club) and being given a training schedule, I had to make one of the most difficult decisions in my young life.

The club practice sessions included Wednesday afternoons and concluded in the evenings. However, my church's prayer meetings were also on Wednesday evenings. This, of course, quickly became a problem because I began to miss prayer meetings. I was summoned to a meeting by my church's leadership (meaning I was called on the red carpet, as it was referred to back then).

At that meeting, I was reprimanded for missing prayer meetings and then presented with two choices: I was told I had to make a choice between serving the Lord and being an athlete.

> *"I call heaven and earth to witness against you today, that I have set before you, life and death, the blessing and the curse. So, choose life in order that you may live, you and your descendants." Deuteronomy 30:19 (NASB)*

For many years, that meeting left an indelible mark on my mind, which made it hard for me to forget that evening's event. I loved the Lord, but I also loved being an athlete. Remember, I had been running since I was in primary school and was known for being an athlete. But you know what – I also knew that I loved the Lord, and I loved being a Christian even though I was not always behaving as one.

Do you recall how in the beginning of this book, I spoke about always fighting? Well, while attending high school, I was involved in fewer fights than before. I think my fights were only in the first year of high school. Not that I became a saint or anything, but now I accepted the fact that I was a child of God and knew I had to live and behave differently.

> *"Direct my footsteps according to your word; let no sin rule over me." Psalm 119:133 (NIV)*

Granted, my life had changed, but I still loved sports – and here I was in a meeting with these leaders who I deemed to be super spiritual asking me to make what I considered to be a terrible choice. Although the rest of the meeting is somewhat blurry now, I left having made the decision to follow the Lord. So that was the end of my athletic career. Oh, how times have changed!

Like many of you, I experienced turbulent times as I navigated high school. But whatever I went through, encountered, or had to face in those formative stages of my teenage life, l learned this: the choices I make in life are like stepping stones to life's final destination.

Unfortunately, many of us wait until we are in the valley of decisions, or in the midst of a crisis, before we even consider what our choices should be. There is no preparation; we tend to go through life with no consideration or contemplation of the "what ifs."

Considering our choices does not mean that we are not trusting in the Lord; it simply means that we are preparing ourselves for any eventuality so we can pray accordingly.

The Bible admonishes us to trust in God:

> *"Have I not commanded you? Be strong and courageous. Do not be frightened, and do not be dismayed, for the Lord your God is with you wherever you go." Joshua 1:9 (ESV)*

> *"Trust in the Lord with all your heart, and do not lean on your own understanding. In all your ways acknowledge him, and he will make straight your paths." Proverbs 3:5-6 (ESV)*

Too many of us never realize that the bad things of our past were preparing us for the good things in our future. If we ignore our past, then the lessons learned cannot propel us into our desired futures. In our formative years, the very thought of making decisions that would ultimately affect our lives after high school was probably unnerving and intimidating.

Those adolescent years were when our brain and emotions were seemingly in constant cahoots; the tendency was to question and second-guess ourselves more often than we normally would.

We sought to predict what our lives would look like or be like after high school. Would college be an option or not? Could we even begin to pay for it? But if we knew then what we know now, we would have opted to lean on the Lord, though that may surprise us to realize. He is the only one who knows our end from the beginning and has the ability to chart our course, if we allow Him. For He said:

"It is the Lord your God you must follow, and him you must revere. Keep his commands and obey him; serve him and hold fast to him. Deuteronomy 13:4 (NIV)

"I know the plans I have for you, declares the Lord, plans for welfare and not for evil, to give you a future and a hope." Jeremiah 29:11 (ESV)

The Lord has already set us up for success. It is up to us as individuals to determine what that success would look like. David rightly says in Psalm 23:

"Even if I go through the deepest darkness, I will not be afraid, Lord, for you are with me. Your shepherd's rod and staff protect me." Psalm 23:4 (GNT)

Chapter 3
Come Walk With Me

The Call and Glimpses of Missionary Training

"In everything we do, we show that we are true ministers of God. We patiently endure troubles and hardships and calamities of every kind." 2 Corinthians 6:4 (NLT)

"Do your best to present yourself to God as one approved, a worker who does not need to be ashamed and who correctly handles the word of truth." 2 Timothy 2:15 (NIV)

After being involved in church work and many positions of leadership for many years, in 1976 I entered what was then the Full Gospel Missionary Training Center. I had felt called to the ministry many years before but had decided I was not ready. After high school, a friend got me a job as a teacher in a private school. I loved teaching, but there was a constant battle in my head about attending Bible school.

There were situations I needed to consider: my sister had been the sole breadwinner supporting the family for many years, and I knew the very thought of quitting my job for Bible school would seem unconscionable to her. Also, I had secured an interview with a community high school during that time. However, on the afternoon of the interview I realized I could not go.

> *"Whoever does not take his cross and follow me is not worthy of me." Matthew 10:38 (ESV)*

During that entire day at work, I was wrestling with my thoughts and emotions, and I had made the decision that I was going to Bible school. Then I had to go home and tell my mother and sister about my decision. I remember entering the house and my mom asking me how the interview went, and me telling her I did not go. She held her head and said she did not want to know, so that she could tell my sister when she got home from work that she had no idea what I had done.

We were both aware that there was going to be a problem when my sister learned that I had not gone for the interview. So, needless to say, my sister was furious when she got home and found out. I remember her crying and saying it was so unfair, while I tried explaining what was happening in my heart. But eventually, despite her objections, I left home for Bible school.

> *"Blessed are all who fear the Lord, who walk in obedience to him." Psalm 128:1 (NIV)*

The thought of attending Bible school gave me a kind of euphoric feeling. I was entering a place filled with people who loved the Lord, and it was going to be a glorious three years, or so I thought. I soon discovered that I was in the midst of human beings who loved the Lord but were still flawed, some more than others.

In the bigger scheme of things, everyone was undoubtedly called into ministry, but many were working out their individual issues just like I was. We were living by faith, trusting God to provide our needs (we were a self-supporting body).

Due to my responsibilities at my church, I was allowed to go home on weekends. My mom would stock me up with baked goods and homemade drinks to take back with me on Mondays, which my roommates could not wait to enjoy.

There were many things I did not expect to be doing in Bible school. One would think that we were there to study the scriptures in order to "rightly divide the word of truth" (2 Timothy 2:15). It was a rude awakening when I realized that there was manual labor involved.

Some students were required to work in the building department completing the dormitories, and others were assigned to different departments. Depending on the department we were in, some of us had duties in the mornings before class and then again in the afternoons, while some only had afternoon work.

As for me, I worked in various departments. I started out in the pineapple field, planting pineapples and keeping the area free from weeds. Then I became the leader of a team that worked in the cow pen (oh, how I loved my cows). The cows all had names, and I can see them even today in my mind's eye, remembering how they would come running as I called their names.

We had a calf that I called Skinny because he was like skin and bones when we got him. He knew his name so well. He would be grazing in the field, and I would stand at the door of the cow pen and shout, "Skinny!" and he would come running. We fed him milk from a baby's bottle until he was able to eat by himself.

Then there was Molly, the largest cow in the group, but also the gentlest. She was so tall that I could not see over her, yet it was as though she appreciated being looked after. At feeding time, she would step aside for us to put down her bucket of feed, unlike the others who could not wait to get their mouths in the buckets.

There was Patsy, who, interestingly, I had named after myself. I don't know if this was animal imitating man, but she was unruly. She was actually responsible for kicking me in the head and giving me a concussion. My tenure in the cow pen taught me a lot. The cows had personalities just like people, so I learned them and acted accordingly.

After a while, I was put in charge of ordering supplies for all the departments: the kitchen, garden, pig, chicken, and cow, to name a few. This meant that I was responsible for handling thousands of dollars. What I was most proud of was that every month, I was able to account for every dollar entrusted to me, and I was praised for being so efficient. I never realized that this was preparation for my life after Bible school.

"If you are faithful in little things, you will be faithful in large ones. But if you are dishonest in

little things, you won't be honest with greater responsibilities." Luke 16:10 (NLT)

During my years in Bible school, I came to understand who I was. I had always been a no-nonsense person, even as a child. I spoke my mind and was allowed to express myself without being muzzled. Bible school, I soon realized, allowed some people to live a wannabe, artificial life. Many tried to project this "holier than thou" attitude. Of course, we all came from different backgrounds, countries, and cultures. But the need to be someone else spiritually seemed to be the order of the day.

It stands to reason, therefore, that I stuck out like a sore thumb. Conformity was never part of my nature. I was that individual who needed to always know why. This did not endear me to many, but I loved the Lord and knew I was where I needed to be. I was accused of being a few things – worldly, proud, know-it-all, etc. – but when my pastor said he needed to speak with me one Sunday after church, that was a different story.

That meeting was one to remember. My pastor knew me quite well, so he prefaced the meeting by saying, "Ingi, I know this is not true, but this is what I was told." I was being accused of reading sex books, and supposedly because of that, one of my roommates was being attacked by demons. Needless to say, I was livid.

"If your brother sins against you, go and tell him his fault, between you and him alone. If he listens to you, you have gained your brother." Matthew 18:15 (ESV)

You see, I was an avid reader from since a young age; I believe this is where my extensive vocabulary comes from (I am not just tooting my own horn). My professors at Georgia State University loved my writings, and one even suggested I become a professor. Would you believe it if I told you that the first time, I watched a movie or saw a television show was when I was 24 years old? That movie was The Six Million Dollar Man (The Bionic Man) in black and white, which I saw while I was attending a conference in Suriname.

What troubled me most about that conversation with my pastor was not only that I was being accused of something that was entirely false, but that it was reported to my pastor without first speaking with me. This was wrong on two levels: the young lady should have spoken with me before going to the leadership, and the leader should have spoken with me before going to my pastor. The scriptures say:

> "A single witness shall not rise up against a man on account of any iniquity or sin which he has committed; on the evidence of two or three witnesses a matter shall be confirmed." Deuteronomy 19:15 (NASB)

This definitely did not happen in the way the Bible instructs. I mentioned this to my pastor and expressed how disappointed I was with the entire situation.

That following Monday on my return to Bible school, I immediately made an appointment to meet with our superintendent. At that meeting, I expressed my disappointment with the way the accusation was handled and how it was contrary to scripture (as if he didn't know). I then stated that the accusation was entirely false, and the book I was reading was a Mills & Boon novel I'd gotten in a book exchange from one of his daughters. Shocker! Then everything took on a different light.

Fast forward to our reunion many years later, where I was approached by my supposed accuser, who told me she was so happy to see me because for years she wanted to get the opportunity to apologize to me for that situation (she had left Bible school before graduation). Without going into too much detail, I was happy to learn that what had been presented to me at the time was not what she had actually said. I must confess, though, that all the while I'd had an inclination that what I was being told was not entirely true. It seemed that throughout Bible school, we were told things that were used to keep us "in check."

I graduated from Bible school in the class of 1980 and was ordained as a missionary. Interestingly, the female graduates were all missionaries while the male graduates had specific five-fold ministry "callings." Does this ring a bell, anyone?

Through it all, I realized the things we do and the decisions we make earlier in life can never fully prepare us for how we envision things in our lives would ultimately be. There will definitely be ups and downs, because everything that we desire is worth fighting for. The things we face and the people we encounter can have both positive and negative effects on us, but what matters most is how we allow these encounters to shape our lives. Ultimately, we are all responsible for our own actions.

There were times when I literally had to decide if I was going to cut and run or remain committed to the path I had chosen.

> *"Therefore, my dear brothers and sisters, stand firm. Let nothing move you. Always give yourselves fully to the work of the Lord, because you know that your labor in the Lord is not in vain." 1 Corinthians 15:58 (NIV)*

It was no joke; this was a real pressure for me because I could not readily conform to things and situations without understanding why it was required. I understood that I was in a Christian community, but I always had to know why certain things were done, whether I deemed them right or wrong. I was never able to follow anyone or anything blindly. Of course, one should never just be a follower for following's sake. There must be a purpose in your decision. Even the Scriptures admonish us:

> *"But in your hearts revere Christ as Lord. Always be prepared to give an answer to everyone who asks you to give the reason for the hope that you have. But do this with gentleness and respect. 1 Peter 3:15 (NIV)*

Looking back, I might not have followed the last sentence in that verse every time. Perhaps I missed it more often than not. Oh, how I have grown! Not of my own doing, but I eventually understood that it was tiresome to always be in a fighting reactive mode. **"Let go and let God"** is more than a cliché, it revolutionized my life – and believe me when I say it can revolutionize yours too. I read somewhere, *"it is not what you are that holds you back;*

it is what you think you are not," and *"you cannot always control circumstances, but you can always control your own thoughts."*

> *"As he thinks within himself, so he is."* Proverbs 23:7 (NASB)

The entire chapter of Proverbs 23 speaks of how to react in certain situations. So, what about you? How have you handled situations when doing the right thing backfired, and what you thought was right ended up giving you a backlash?

Making decisions can be a very difficult process, so how and when can we know we are making the right choices? The answer is the decision or path that leads us to peace of mind. If after you have made a decision, you feel conflicted, step back and re-evaluate. I want us to be reminded that we are never alone in this process. Jesus promised to always be by our sides.

> *"If you wander off the road to the right or the left, you will hear his voice behind you saying, 'Here is the road. Follow it.'"* Isaiah 30:21 (GNT)

Overview of Relationships and Marriage

Prior to getting married, I was in two relationships. The first one was a relationship of convenience. I lived a distance from church and a group of us would walk home together, and before I realized it, I was in a relationship.

Don't get me wrong, he was a very good person and very

good to me; but even though I was young, I knew I would not and could not marry him. I even told my mother and sister that. He had a bicycle that I would sometimes use to go to school. Looking back years later, I knew I was wrong to do that because he loved me. Writing this book makes me want to tell him I am sorry for leading him on – I don't remember if I ever did.

The second relationship I had was with someone I would call my first love, and I knew I was also his first love. We received the blessing of our pastor for the relationship, but because of his position in the church, we tried to keep the relationship private. However, others suspected and some had even seen us together.

This was a roller coaster kind of a relationship. We so wanted to please God, and the "will of God" was such a driving force in our lives back then that we fluctuated between believing our relationship was of God one day and not being sure the next day.

One day, as I was going about my business, I saw my boyfriend and the superintendent conversing under the mechanic shed. I thought for an instant that it was strange he was there, because I had no idea he was coming. Apparently, unbeknownst to me, he was there to discuss our relationship.

To add insult to injury, later that day, the superintendent of the Bible school told me to leave the man of God alone, to which I responded with my regular quick comeback, "I thought it took two persons to be in a relationship." I understood why this was said; my boyfriend at this point was seen as "up and coming" in the organization.

This, however, is not what ended our relationship. When we were on, the relationship was fabulous, but that pressure to be in the perfect will of God eventually took its toll, and we agreed to end the relationship and go our separate ways. However, we have remained good friends.

On September 2, 1980, I said "I do" to the love of my life, Richard L.B. Conliffe, after two and a half years in a long-distance relationship. I met my husband while in Bible school. We were having our annual International Christian Leadership Connections (ICLC) conference, which was being followed by two weddings. Both of the young ladies were marrying Aruban men, and my future husband's nephew was one of them. He was there with a few other family members for the weddings.

During the conference, the Bible school students were servers, and every time I was serving, I would notice this young man looking at me. I paid no attention to him because I did not want it said that I was after a foreigner. However, at the end of the conference, on a Friday night after dinner, my friend Phyllis and I were walking to our dorm.

Suddenly, this same young man came running up behind us. He said hi and introduced himself, saying his name was Richard but folks called him Richie. We introduced ourselves in turn, and he asked if we were going to the first wedding the following day. We replied that we were, and he responded, "I'll see you tomorrow, then."

As we continued walking to the dorm, my girlfriend said, "From now on, I will call you 'Sister R.'" "Sister R?" I responded, definitely baffled. "R for whom?" I had forgotten the guy had just said his name was Richie. She answered, "R for Richie," and I busted out laughing, telling her she was crazy because we had just met the guy. I guess she was being prophetic!

The following day at the wedding, Richie and I spent some time talking. Then he went and got a flower from I don't know where, and he stuck it in my hair. I looked around, and there were some unpleasant looks glaring in our direction. I thought to myself that this was exactly the thing I was afraid of – folks thinking I was running after a foreigner.

The next Saturday was Richie's nephew's wedding, and again I was in attendance. This time I tried to be strategic and sat next to a male friend, making sure there was not an empty seat next to me. Across from me sat three of the Bible school superintendent's daughters. My male friend got up to get something to drink, and before I could even blink, Richie was sitting in the guy's seat. I whispered, "We don't do things like this." By this time, all eyes were on us, and I could only imagine what the girls would tell their dad and what he would think.

You see, I was still in that relationship I spoke about. Now fast forward to Richie entering the picture. After the wedding fiasco, Richie returned to Aruba and started writing me, asking to be my boyfriend. But remember, I was in this other relationship. Richie's letters kept coming, and I was having a problem with them, because although I understood what he was saying, his tenses and grammar were all over the place. I really could not see myself in a relationship with him – and again, I had this other person who I loved.

I had a very good girlfriend, Dawn, who was always able to be my sense of reason in Bible school whenever I had an issue. I would share Richie's letters with her and comment on the sentence construction and everything else. She would always caution me to be careful.

Richie was relentless in pursuing me and asking me to be his girlfriend. Eventually, I told the other individual I could no longer go on with our uncertainties because there was someone else interested in me, and we ended the relationship. At this point, I was not yet in love with Richie, but because of his persistence, I decided to pray about it. I can remember one day as I was praying, telling the Lord I had no love for Richie, but if this was the person, he had to give me a love for him. It stands to reason; the rest is history.

Over the years, I have counseled young women about relationships. I realize everyone, male and female, wants the best person on their arm. This means that many times, for the price of beauty or status, couples who are not compatible in any way walk down the aisle in marriage. I am not talking about the fact that opposites attract. I am addressing the fact that many embark in holy matrimony knowing full well that they are not giving a hundred percent to the impending union.

Unfortunately, this can even be seen in the church setting. Seemingly, everyone wants to marry a pastor, and pastors want to marry a beautiful first lady – hence the despicable statistics for church and Christian marriages. Of course, there are exceptions; no one should stay in an abusive relationship for any reason.

This year (2020) will be our 40th wedding anniversary. Was it always smooth? No, not really, especially when early in our marriage, someone I considered a friend tried to infiltrate our marriage bond. During that time, I truly came to recognize what true commitment was and how much my husband loves me.

Thereafter, I became watchful and cautious, and I never opened the door for that to happen again. As women, we tend to share how wonderful our husbands are, and how well we are being treated and taken care of, never realizing how what we are saying is affecting the listener. I hold no grudge and have forgiven.

I challenge you right now with this question: Who is it that you need to forgive? Say that name or names out loud. Does it seem that the incident, whatever it was, has left a lasting impression on your mind, and try as you might, you can't get over it? Ask the Holy Spirit to bring you release if you are struggling with unforgiveness. Know this day is your day of deliverance. Victory is here, right now, right this hour, right this minute. Take hold of it. Christ has forgiven us; so, ought we to forgive. Embrace the word of God and repeat it daily.

> *"Bear with each other and forgive one another if any of you has a grievance against someone. Forgive as the Lord forgave you." Colossians 3:13 (NIV)*

> *"Get rid of all bitterness, rage and anger, brawling and slander, along with every form of malice. Be kind and compassionate to one another, forgiving each other, just as in Christ*

God forgave you." Ephesians 4:31-32 (NIV)

Everything we go through in life can prepare us for the next chapters if we allow God to take control. With Him at the helm, He turns our mourning into dancing.

"Thou hast turned for me my mourning into dancing: thou hast put off my sackcloth, and girded me with gladness." Psalm 30:11 (KJV)

Birth of My Children

Children are life's greatest blessings.

"Behold, children are a heritage from the Lord, the fruit of the womb a reward. Like arrows in the hand of a warrior are the children of one's youth. Blessed is the man who fills his quiver with them! He shall not be put to shame when he speaks with his enemies in the gate." Psalm 127:3-5 (ESV)

"Train up a child in the way he should go; even when he is old, he will not depart from it." Proverbs 22:6 (ESV)

Enough cannot be said about the joy and sense of completeness children bring to a marriage and family. Whether that family was created through natural births or adoptions, there is that undeniable sense of bonding that is inexplicable. Of course, raising children comes with its challenges, but being a parent is one of the most rewarding privileges one could ever have.

Children are also a representation of our relationship with God; the love we shower them with exemplifies and mirrors the heavenly Father's love for us. My husband had always said he wanted five children. He had eleven siblings; I, on the other hand, have only two. I had thought that three children would be enough, but I conceded to him wanting five.

On September 1, 1981, one day before our first anniversary a beautiful baby girl was added to our family – Montra Anastasia. She was such a beautiful baby and slept through the night from the very first day we brought her home from the hospital.

It was about two years into our marriage that I suffered a miscarriage. I remember having pains during the day but having to teach a class that Wednesday night at church, and so I decided to go, even though my mom told me not to. I was in excruciating pain.

On my return home, I went to use the bathroom and the fetus fell out on the bathroom floor. I remember thinking, "This looks like a rat." My mom helped clean me up and I went to bed. I was in pain for a while, and then the pain subsided. I can't really remember if we told anyone outside our immediate family.

> *"So with you; now is your time of grief, but I will see you again and you will rejoice, and no one will take away your joy." John 16:22 (NIV)*

Two years later, I became pregnant again. Because of the size of my tummy, I was constantly being told that I was having a boy. We considered names for boys and chose

Fabian. My husband was excited because he wanted a boy, but more importantly, we did not want to know beforehand – no gender reveal parties back then!

We had always purchased gender neutral baby clothes. Each pregnancy we wanted to be surprised, and surprised we were when I delivered a beautiful baby girl instead of the boy, we thought we were having. On April 1, 1985, Fabian Alawtricia was born.

As I said, we already had a name for a boy, and after I gave birth, we decided we were going to keep the name Fabian. At that time, we had no idea that it could be a unisex name. Fabian, like her sister, slept through the night the first day we bought her home. At this point, we had never had crying babies. I guess they both had their father's temperament – quiet and relaxed.

One day after this, I started having a slight pain in my abdomen. As time went on, the pain intensified. I was working in the timeshare industry at the time, and the hotel guests would tell me it was probably my appendix. I would have to sit a lot because the pain made it difficult to stand. My doctor had no idea what was wrong and was giving me lots of pain pills.

I remember Richie calling a friend over one night because I was screaming in pain. She came over and prayed, but it seemed as if prayers weren't working. We had no idea what was going on, and I was in terrible agony. Every move produced excruciating pain. At this point, I had suffered with the abdominal pain for about three months.

"In the same way, the Spirit helps us in our

weakness. We do not know what we ought to pray for, but the Spirit himself intercedes for us through wordless groans." Romans 8:26 (NIV)

One day as I was home alone, I heard a sound outside. I looked through my bedroom window and saw a church sister of mine, Carol. She was driving a car and declared she had contacted a specialist and was taking me to see him. By the time we got there, the pain had become unbearable; I had difficulty getting out of the car. Surprisingly, the specialist was standing at the office door waiting for me.

As I entered the office, he directed me to a room and told me to lie on a table. As I sat on the edge of the table, I attempted to lie down and immediately screamed because it was as if something was ripping apart in my abdomen. The specialist checked me briefly and said I needed to go to the hospital immediately. He called the hospital and told them I was on my way. He took care of everything on the phone.

"So shalt thou find favor and good understanding in the sight of God and man." Proverbs 3:4 (KJV)

When we got to the hospital I was admitted, and later that evening, they advised me that I was going to be prepped for an 8 a.m. surgery. All the while, I had no idea what was happening. When my husband came to the hospital, I told him they were just going to check what was going on with me. In our naivety, we did not ask the right questions. To our surprise, the following morning I underwent major surgery.

After the surgery I was returned to my room. When I awoke, it was then I learned that I had major surgery because I had an ectopic pregnancy (a pregnancy in the fallopian tube). No one told me any of this, not even the doctor, who knew exactly why I was having surgery. Needless to say, when I was allowed to walk later that evening, I called my mom and my sister. My sister was furious, saying no one undergoes major surgery without notifying the family. I explained we had no idea I was having major surgery.

My mom had been away visiting my sister in the United States, and she returned within the next two days to take care of me. What was amazing and praiseworthy throughout this entire episode was the fact that I carried a baby in my fallopian tube for over three months and lived. The medical staff was in disbelief because my fallopian tube should have ruptured long before, but God, Hallelujah!

> *"Have mercy on me, my God, have mercy on me, for in you I take refuge. I will take refuge in the shadow of your wings until the disaster has passed." Psalm 57:1 (NIV)*

On the follow-up visit with the specialist, he again expressed that my carrying the baby in the fallopian tube for so long was unbelievable. We were then told that the possibility of me getting pregnant again was slim to none, because I now had only one fallopian tube. Remember, this is over 33 years ago; medicine was much less advanced then. Though the news was discouraging, we accepted it. My mom did not help matters, though, because she was insisting that the lost baby was the boy my husband had always wanted.

By God's grace, I became pregnant again two years later. This was now my fifth pregnancy. We were excited because what the doctors said was impossible had happened. On October 23, 1989, our son Richard-Harvey was born. I did not realize how much pressure my husband was under to produce a boy until his response to the doctor saying, "Congratulations, it's a boy" – he blurted out, "That can't change, right?" Everyone in the room started laughing. Richard-Harvey's arrival completed our family.

> *"Understand, therefore, that the Lord your God is indeed God. He is the faithful God who keeps his covenant for a thousand generations and lavishes his unfailing love on those who love him and obey his commands." Deuteronomy 7:9 (NLT)*

We were a happy and contented family. Our family unit was tight and close. We enjoyed traveling together, and the children loved it. This was something neither their father nor I ever did. To this day, it is always nice to listen to them reminiscing about their childhood.

We gave the kids everything they needed, wanted, and more. Coming from single-parent households, I believe we overcompensated for that. Some folks said our children were spoiled because they grew up with helpers in the home. Would I do some things differently today? Perhaps, but we enjoyed doing it back then.

> *"Hear, my son, your father's instruction, and*

forsake not your mother's teaching, for they are a graceful garland for your head and pendants for your neck." Proverbs 1:8-9 (ESV)

God was good to us and blessed our endeavors. I was very successful in my job, and we showed our gratitude to the Lord by being faithful tithers and givers. The more our heavenly Father blessed us, the more we gave. Even before I was married, I knew giving was going to be an integral part of my ministry. I had no money back then, but I knew instinctively that it would happen. God gave me a husband who is of the same persuasion, and we just love to give and help others. It brings us such joy that we are in a position to give. Being a blessing to the body of Christ is so rewarding. We taught our children to give and instilled in them from a very young age the fact that we can never out-give God.

"Honor the Lord with your wealth, with the firstfruits of all your crops." Proverbs 3:9 (NIV)

"Give, and it will be given to you. A good measure, pressed down, shaken together and running over, will be poured into your lap. For with the measure you use, it will be measured to you." Luke 6:38 (NIV)

Each of us has a different life story, but we all face storms or tumultuous occasions at one time or another. It is the decisions we make as we go through challenges that determine how we come out on the other side.

Chapter 4
Life's Storm

Friendship Hurt

"There are 'friends' who destroy each other, but a real friend sticks closer than a brother."
Proverbs 18:24 (NLT)

After living in Aruba for a little while, one evening I was invited to the home of one of the sisters. I thought we were all friends because we had all been in Bible school together except for one person. Now, I was oblivious to what the gathering was about; you can imagine my surprise when I realized that I was going to be the topic of conversation at the gathering. Remember, I am living on a strange island with my husband; the small family I had was back in Guyana. So apart from my husband, the only other people I knew were these folks who had attended the Bible school in Guyana with me.

At this gathering, I was "roasted," in today's language. I was treated with such disdain that it was unconscionable, especially coming from a group of Christian women. I was told that no one liked me because I thought I was sophisticated and folks were having difficulty understanding me because I was using too many "big" words. This was astonishing to me because I had not changed my speech. I was speaking the way I had always spoken to them. Then I was reprimanded for wearing gold chains, and told I was causing the young people to stumble. I told them the long chain was the last thing my mom gave me when I was leaving Guyana, and my husband had bought the one with my initials in diamonds, but that fact fell on deaf ears.

"Do to others as you would have them do to you." Luke 6:31 (NIV)

I told them that if they had really known me, they would have known that I had no aversion to wearing jewelry but had refrained because it was frowned upon in Guyana. No one was ever able to convincingly explain to me over the years from the scriptures why wearing jewelry was wrong. I had always told anyone who would listen that I would wear jewelry if and when I left Guyana. It stood to reason that that was what I was doing.

If I was expecting any kind of sympathy, that thought quickly flew out the window as I was being ridiculed. I was even told folks were asking why my husband had married me when there were beautiful girls in Aruba. "Need I explain?" I thought. I had learned a long time ago that it is the answer that causes the most problems, so I let that statement go unchallenged. Many more hurtful things were said that there is no reason to reiterate here.

When I left that gathering, I cried all the way home because I felt all alone and like an outsider. When I got home, my husband asked how the gathering was, and I started crying even more. Those who know me can attest to the fact that I am not a crier. Seeing that I was so much in tears, my husband readily recognized that something had gone terribly wrong.

After composing myself, I was able to relate to him what had transpired. My husband was furious. This was out of character because he is such a quiet, laid-back person, but that night he was my knight in shining armor. He said, and I quote, "I am your husband, and if I say you can wear jewelry no one else can tell you differently, so you are not going to take those chains off," and I never did.

Someone once said, "Friendship is not about whom you have known the longest. It's about who came and never left your side." Have you found that person that you can truly say is your friend, who is that support system for you? I am happy that today I can say I have some true friends.

Of course, there are those who say they are my friends, but I never ever do anything with them, hardly ever even speak with them on the phone. What type of friendship is that? It sounds more like an acquaintance to me. Friendship is interactive; it does not always have to be constant physical presence, but if you have a friend and you are almost never in contact, I am sorry to say, but that is an acquaintance.

There are times in friendships when there are disagreements, when things don't go your way, but the commitment to the bond of friendship is still there. If you are unable to speak with your "friend" for months on end, you might as well just choose to speak with your dog. Such folks should be moved to the acquaintance zone. You still love them, but you must accept the fact that is all they will ever be to you. True friendship is nourished and cultivated over time.

> *"A friend loves at all times, and a brother is born for a time of adversity." Proverbs 17:17 (NIV)*

> *"As iron sharpens iron, so one person sharpens another" Proverbs 27:17 (NIV)*

Church Hurt

> *"The Lord is close to the brokenhearted and saves those who are crushed in spirit." Psalm 34:18 (NIV)*

Any kind of pain in life is very hurtful, no matters if it is physical pain or emotional pain, and no two people's pain is alike. The fact is, we have all experienced pain at some point, but we all process it differently. Because some hurts can be seen in the form of a physical injury, most times we can quickly eradicate it with medication. But there are hurts that reside deep within our physique and our hearts that only we know about, and only the Holy Spirit can soothe and heal them.

Experiencing church hurt is like no other. One would presuppose that the church is a safe place. After all, it is the place where we call each other brother and sister. Nothing, however, can be further from the truth. Some of the times I have experienced being hurt the most were in church settings with church folks. Not to paint all Christians with the same brush, but it is unfortunate that though we love each other, many feel their positions are threatened with talented individuals around.

Unfortunately, in today's world, because many do not understand their purpose (even though they say they do), their need to vie for position and be recognized seems to be their driving force.

For me, being hurt manifested itself in various situations. An incident occurred when I was attending a concert. Our church had a beautiful singing group, and there would be concerts periodically. My understanding of Christianity from conversion meant that I represented the King, so it was always important for me to dress like a child of the King. Unfortunately, many perceived my style of dressing to be "worldly." Back then, and to this day I love looking and dressing beautiful whenever I go out. I was looking for a seat, and my husband was across the way when I crossed paths with a leader who said something to me. I sat down and started crying uncontrollably – yes, me!

To this day I can't remember what he said, but I can remember how it made me feel. Then this quote by Eleanor Roosevelt popped into my mind: *"No one can make you feel inferior without your consent."* I had no recollection of ever having heard the quote before. It was as if the Holy Spirit downloaded it into my spirit. I stopped crying immediately, dried my tears, and have never allowed anyone since that day to make me feel inferior. When we got home, I researched that statement to see if it was correct.

That night changed my life forever. I realized that I was in a new place with a fairly new partner for life. Still, it was imperative that I find out who I was and how I was going to function in this whole new environment. I discovered who I am, and I walk in it unapologetically. For those of you who think I am cocky, I apologize, but this is the God-given confidence I have had since then and still walk in. In fact, my friends say I command a room whenever I enter.

Another incident taught me what real leadership should be. I had been the worship team leader and worship leader at my church for years, as well as a Bible school and new believer's class teacher, and there came a point where I was probably burned out. I had no idea what was happening, but I felt I wanted nothing to do with anything. I was suffering alone and felt I had no one to confide in. I tried explaining what was happening to me to my husband, but he could not understand. To him, I was this strong individual and everything was dandy.

It is said that "hurting people hurt people"; I was hurting and felt I had no resolve. I drafted a letter of resignation from all responsibilities at my church and asked to be transferred to another church, leaving my husband and children at my present church. My intent was not actually to resign, but to generate a meeting with the leadership to express what was happening with me. However, that intention backfired greatly when I was handed a letter in the church yard by the assistant pastor. The letter was signed by the pastor and board members accepting my resignation.

WHAT? I could not believe this was happening. I had served this church faithfully in many different capacities over the years, and all I was worth was a letter shoved in my hand in the church yard. No one in leadership even thought of speaking with me to find out what was happening and why. That situation caused me right then and there to think of the type of leader I would not be. There was no empathy; it felt inhumane that I would be treated that way. I made the determination that when situations arise, I must not only look at the action but to also try to decipher the "why." I was hurting and needed someone in leadership to ask me why.

The experience also taught me that I was really responsible for my brothers and sisters. I am truly my brother's keeper. I contemplated on the many who had walked away from the church. My thought process was that they were probably just like me: reaching out and wanting a listening ear, but finding no empathy and instead being shown or helped to the door. After a year's hiatus at the other church, I rejoined my family at the previous church.

It behooves us in this life to treat others the way we would like to be treated. Possessing the need to hurt and belittle another in order to feel bigger or better about one's own self is in and of itself pathetic. It matters not our socio-economic status, our backgrounds, the color of our skin, our nationality, or anything else. We are all God's creation, living on this earth with specific obligations. None is more superior than the other. We were all created in His image and likeness.

Despite the situations we face, our heavenly Father admonishes us to:

"Come unto me, all of you who are weary and

carry heavy burdens, and I will give you rest."
Matthew 11:28 (NLT)

It is also important to note that the way we may be treated by others does not define who we are. What are some of the hurts you are carrying as a child of God in the church arena? Remember, Joseph is a prime example of how we should not allow the actions of family members and others to define us. Joseph was betrayed by his own brothers, thrown in a pit, and sold to the Ishmaelites (Genesis 37:12-28), then falsely accused by Potiphar's wife (Genesis 39:7-20) and forgotten by the chief cupbearer (Genesis 39:21 – 40:23), yet Joseph never forgot his dreams.

What has God spoken to you over the years, what promises has He made to you, or what kinds of impressions have you felt? As you take inventory of your life, is it all you expect it to be? Are you allowing the hurts you have experienced or are experiencing to be your life's defining story? Don't lose heart, there is no need, just respond to your heavenly Father's call and come out of the "rain." He wants to enfold you in His arms and hold you close to his bosom.

Relationship Hurt

"Be completely humble and gentle; be patient, bearing with one another in love." Ephesians 4:2 (NIV)

"Above all, love each other deeply, because love covers over a multitude of sins." 1 Peter 4:8 (NIV)

Every one of us would relish having healthy relationships – that is a given. Life has taught us that if a relationship is not properly defined, it could cause lots of heartache. It must be noted, however, that this does not only include intimate relationships. There are many platonic relationships that have stood the test of time; these are relationships void of sexual or physical desire but with genuine love and respect for each other.

Over the years, I have mistakenly considered some individuals, both male and female, to be my friends, only to discover that what I thought was a great, healthy platonic relationship was entirely one-sided. It is hard to comprehend how I could have been so gullible and oblivious to the dynamics of some of those relationships. I really wanted these relationships to work because I was in a strange place with not many friends.

All my friends were from Christian circles, so I held on to relationships that were destined to fail from the outset. I was putting in the effort for viable relationships but realized I was wasting my time and energy. I knew intuitively that some of these relationships were questionable, but I would always shrug it off.

> *"Walk with the wise and become wise, for a companion of fools suffers harm." Proverbs 13:20 (NIV)*

In this world, I have found out – to my own detriment, I might add – that there are many people who are conniving. Their life purpose seems to be to use and take advantage of others. I remember reaching out to someone I thought I had a great relationship with for weeks without a response. Eventually I got a call back and was given an explanation for the hiatus.

You can imagine my surprise when I was on Facebook one day and saw the real reason for the absence -the individual was establishing a foundation I was not privy to. I was hurt because of the deception. Everyone has their own lives to live, but if you choose to consider someone or make someone feel that there is a great relationship there, then the famous line from Polonius in Shakespeare's Hamlet is applicable: *"This above all: to thine own self be true, and it must follow, as the night the day, thou canst not then be false to any man."*

I have always had a heart to give, and because of this, some people were nice to me only when they wanted something. Hypocrisy in any form is repulsive, and when used to take advantage of someone, it becomes selfish. I had to allow myself to accept that with some individuals, there was never going to be a relationship.

Case in point: I once traveled a far distance and spent a lot of money to be of support to someone, then I sat dumbfounded in the gathering as I became aware of situations that I was unaware of. Things were being shared that this person I thought I had a great relationship with never told me. Wow! I thought, "This cannot be happening." I returned home and shared what transpired with my family. We decided we would still do our part and continued to be of help and support to that individual.

"Be completely humble and gentle; be patient, bearing with one another in love. Make every effort to keep the unity of the Spirit through the

bond of peace." Ephesians 4:2-3 (NIV)

Then there was the time when we entrusted someone with something very dear to my family and to someone else. After a few years of not realizing anything was amiss, we were alerted by a phone call and then a letter in the mail. We could not believe what we were hearing and reading. We had given full rein to this individual without question before this, perhaps not realizing that accountability is a character trait that cannot be imposed on someone.

Through the grace of God, we were able to count our losses and forgive. The lesson learned was hard and hurtful: trust is like an expensive commodity, and we've got to be mindful of how we use it. We arose like a Phoenix from the ashes of that calamity, but it damaged the relationship and it was never the same.

> *"Do unto others as you would have them do to you." Luke 6:31 (NIV)*

> *"One who has unreliable friends soon comes to ruin, but there is a friend who sticks closer than a brother." Proverbs 18:24 (NIV)*

Unfortunately, it took enduring several more incidents before I came to the realization that if I am the one chasing the dream of making these relationships work, then I am in the relationships all by myself. Eventually I said "Enough is enough" and disregarded those types of relationships. Was I bitter? No, I just took back whatever power I had given to them.

What about you – what types of situations have you had

to endure when you felt you were in a great relationship, but it was draining and demanding and you were not receiving anything in return? I caution you today not to be bitter. Do not allow that experience to cause you to miss out on the pure, genuine relationships that are out there. Ask the heavenly Father to connect you to such people, and He will.

"Above all, love each other deeply, because love covers over a multitude of sins." 1 Peter 4:8 (NIV)

And take comfort in the fact that God is not only your Father but also your friend. He is trustworthy, honorable, dependable, faithful, reliable, constant, steady, and unwavering, that's who He is. Glory!!

"Greater love has no one than this: to lay down one's life for one's friends." John 15:13 (NIV)

"Owe no one anything, except to love each other, for the one who loves another has fulfilled the law." Romans 13:8 (ESV)

Culture Hurt

"There is [now no distinction in regard to salvation] neither Jew nor Greek, there is neither slave nor free, there is neither male nor female; for you [who believe] are all one in Christ Jesus [no one can claim a spiritual superiority]." Galatians 3:28 (AMP)

"Here there is not Greek and Jew, circumcised

and uncircumcised, barbarian, Scythian, slave,
free; but Christ is all, and in all." Colossians
3:11 (ESV)

The dictionary defines culture as being "the customs, arts, social institutions, and achievements of a particular nation, people, or other social group." This includes biases, inclusion, and diversity. When someone refers to having a "culture shock," it means that the individual may have just experienced something that is contrary to what is acceptable in their culture.

It does not always mean that the behavior is repulsive; it could just be different from the viewer's norm. Because of this, the "perpetrator" can then be ostracized and treated like an outcast. This can conjure up demoralizing feelings and cause one to always be in a defensive mode.

My moving to Aruba was a change in culture in many ways. I moved from a country of 83,000 square miles to an island of 69 square miles – from a place where you can choose to be anonymous if you wanted to a place where everyone seems to know everyone else's business.

This was all new to me, so trying to understand why everyone needed to be in my "business" was difficult, and my reaction was not always acceptable. I reiterate, conformity was never a strong point of mine. I have always had my own mindset about everything, which unfortunately caused people in this culture to think I was arrogant.

"You, however, continue in the things you have
learned and become convinced of, knowing from

whom you have learned them." 2 Timothy 3:14 (NASB)

The situation could be the littlest of things, but when it came to me, it seemed to be always magnified a thousand times over. I could recall the youth department having a debate not long after I arrived in Aruba. Now, I was on a debate team in high school (if you know me, I can argue a point just for arguing's sake), so I was excited about taking part in this debate.

The debate had something to do with soul winning, and being the scholar, I was, fresh out of Bible school and all, I was in my element. I remember speaking about the inestimable value of a soul (Bro. Keeshan my evangelism teacher, I made you proud). However, I was not prepared for the backlash.

A few days later, I was told how ungodly my actions were because I was very argumentative (isn't that what a debate is all about?) and that I did not set a good example for the young people. I was flabbergasted – were these people for real, and was I now going to be living in the midst of a group of pseudo-Christians? My understanding of Christianity was always based on scripture. I was never a "do as I say" individual (except when I was called on the red carpet, but then my love for Jesus was in question).

The Bible says the Word of God is like a refiner's fire. That's why I love it.

> *"You made all the delicate, inner parts of my body and knit me together in my mother's womb. Thank you for making me so wonderfully*

complex! Your workmanship is marvelous –
how well I know it." Psalm 139:13-14 (NLT)

I remember once making a statement to a pastor. I was
not trying to be rude, but I was fed up with listening to
peoples' personal conflicts being preached from the
pulpit. I said, "You can preach whatever you want from
the pulpit, but if it does not line up with scripture, I
couldn't be bothered." Was I being pretentious? Definitely
not. I just have a big aversion to leaders using the pulpit
to spew out their own insecurities while badgering and
subjecting believers to unscriptural opinions.

I also know what it is like to be "benched" if it was
perceived that I had done or said something wrong, or if
I expressed my opinion about a matter, or if what I was
propagating was contrary to the status quo. Having an
independent mindset has never endeared me to a lot of
people. I know also what it feels like to be punished as an
adult, and to have what I was doing taken away from me
and given to another. However, it takes a bigger person to
sit back and watch others try to do the things you could
do in your sleep.

God knew exactly what He was doing when He made me.
I am unapologetically me.

> *"The Spirit of God has made me, and the breath*
> *of the Almighty gives me life." Job 33:4 (ESV)*

> *"I knew you before I formed you in your*
> *mother's womb. Before you were born I set you*
> *apart and appointed you as my prophet to the*
> *nations." Jeremiah 1:5 (NLT)*

The truth is, I experienced a lot of hurt over the years while living in Aruba. This might be shocking news to many because of my personality, but if you cut me, I bleed like everyone else. I know I can be intimidating, but to me I am a gentle giant. Was the way I was treated all intentional? I don't really think so; most of it could have been cultural differences. Noticeably, of the entire group I was the one who was totally different. I was cut from a different cloth, and confidence was always what I was clothed in.

> *"Being confident of this very thing, that he which hath begun a good work in you will perform it   until the day of Jesus Christ."* *Philippians 1:6 (KJV)*

I became successful to a certain extent and watched my success be a hindrance to some. Words have no real meaning if they are not followed by the appropriate action. As stated in chapter 3 of this narrative, part of my ministry and calling is to be a giver. Over the years, my family and I have always supported the churches we were a part of. It was painful to watch my brothers and sisters support the unsaved (most of whom by the way, do not return the tithes or give offerings) when I had the same things to offer. Without going into too much detail because my intent is not to hurt anyone, I felt that my giving was appreciated, but I was not supported.

The scripture admonishes:

> *"And let us not be weary in well doing: for in due season we shall reap, if we faint not."* *Galatians 6:9 (KJV)*

Through it all, though, I was never daunted in my resolve to support the kingdom of God. My family says this all the time, and it has become our mantra: *"we can never out-give God."* To God be the glory, He has proven Himself faithful throughout the years.

It is important that as we transition from being consumed by our hurts, our dependency on God becomes greater and stronger. Even His name conjures up unbelievable strength as we call upon Him. Therefore, let's give it all to Him and let go.

> *"The name of the Lord is a fortified tower, the righteous run to it and are safe." Proverbs 18:10 (NIV)*

Chapter 5
Living It All Out

The Power Of Letting Go

How do we let go after we have been taken advantage of, ridiculed, despised, rejected, made fun of, treated as less than, shunned, and called out of our names? This is no easy task; letting go of anything can be a monumental task in and of itself. It is one of the hardest things to do. The decisions we face can be overwhelming because the tendency is to hold on to what has been our protection.

Although we know without a shadow of a doubt that we must let go, at times holding on seems like the better alternative. We begin to rationalize and battle with the fact that there are both good times and bad times in a relationship. Then we pull out our mental scales and begin weighing the good versus the bad scenarios, failing to recognize that letting go is for our own personal benefit.

"So do not fear, for I am with you; do not be dismayed, for I am your God. I will strengthen you and help you; I will uphold you with my righteous right hand." Isaiah 41:10 (NIV)

We must therefore appreciate who we are and accept that things and relationships must sometimes come to an end. The question then becomes, "Where do I begin?" The road ahead seems long and daunting, and we forget the saying, *"A journey of a thousand miles begins with a single step."* Naturally, there must be that beginning point of letting go; it then becomes, "What am I supposed to be letting go of first?" Ironically, we immediately want to tackle the thing that is looming the largest in front of our faces, never stopping to consider how we can tackle the big elm tree if for years we were unable to cut down the little twigs inside of us.

> *"Cast all your anxiety on him because he cares for you."* *1 Peter 5:7 (NIV)*

Part of our natural tendency is to hold on to things that are familiar, even when it takes a death grip to do so. The fear of being alone, not connected, left out, or excluded often seems to be greater than the very thought of letting go for our own sanctity and happiness. The fear of isolation grips us, and suffering is deemed acceptable. We can see the root of this fear in the beginning when the Lord God said:

> *"It is not good for the man to be alone. I will make a helper suitable for him."* *Genesis 2:18 (NIV)*

This was a clear indication that God intended for there to be a community of some sort. It is understandable, therefore, that we struggle when the writing is on the wall for a relationship or friendship to end. Sometimes it feels as if time stands still. The hands of the clock seem not to be moving, and the pendulum swings from one extreme to another in our mind's eye while our mind battles with overwhelming thoughts of loneliness.

It therefore becomes empowering when we muster up the courage and strength to acknowledge the fact that the relationship, situation, employment, or friendship has run its course and come to an end. The difficulty with this is that many believe a relationship, once established, is forever.

Outside of marriage, all other types of relationship can be deemed temporal, in spite of the flood of memories and the weight of emotions we may feel. Granted, the feelings just don't dissipate immediately. However, once the decision is made to leave the relationship, the process becomes somewhat easier.

"He heals the brokenhearted and binds up their wounds." Psalm 147:3 (NIV)

The term "letting go" also encompasses our first being introspective, figuring out how we even allowed ourselves to be in that vulnerable a position. The reasons vary as to why this happens. We should ask ourselves if we are the ones who suction the life out of relationships, or if we are contributing to creating unhealthy relationships by our actions or the things, we are willing to accept.

The onus is on us to be true to our own selves. We know ourselves better that anyone else; therefore, we must recognize when relationships are falling apart or taking a turn to an uncertain end.

None of us, unless we are suicidal, would voluntarily

drive a car off a cliff, or put a gun in our mouths and pull the trigger. If this is true, then we must find it within ourselves to let go of the things or relationships that keep us ensnared. The apostle Paul in his writing to the Hebrews says:

> *"...let us throw off everything that hinders and the sin that so easily entangles..."* Hebrews 12:1 (NIV)

Considering we are already involved; we must now make the choice whether or not we are going to do something about the situation. Of course, there can be outside influences, but ultimately the final decisions always remain ours.

On the flip side, letting go does not have to be all negative. It can also speak to our maturity and the changes occurring in our lives at any given moment. We can be evolving and therefore need to change our relationships, as discussed above. Then there is the environment, our habits, our way of doing things, a job, and the list goes on.

Every year we become a year older; if we choose to, we can also become a year wiser. We have the option to take inventory of our lives and decide what no longer fits. What are the things that are no longer adding or giving value to our lives? Then, as those things are identified, we must proceed to make the adjustments and let them go.

For me, letting go was never a difficult decision – I am a tough cookie! What mattered was how my letting go was going to affect the other individual. As stated before, I had two boyfriends before I got married. Neither relationship was really broadcasted; those who knew, knew and that was that. I remember one of them saying to me many years later that I had the audacity to invite him to my engagement party. But hey, the relationship was over, so why not?

The Bible gives the account of Cain and Abel:

> *"Then the Lord said to Cain, 'Where is your brother Abel?' 'I don't know,' he replied. 'Am I my brother's keeper?'" Genesis 4:9 (NIV)*

"My brother's keeper" refers to the fact that I am responsible for someone else. Unfortunately, Cain's words seem to typify humanity's unwillingness to be culpable for the welfare of their fellow man. I had to learn that it was not always about me; there were others involved.

When we are getting over or letting go of something or someone, the tendency is to only consider ourselves. This is wrong on so many levels. I had to recognize that the other individual needed to "land" in a secure place. If this world is truly going to become a better place, then consideration of others must be paramount.

I have seen individuals and friends who are seemingly in desperate need of friendships and relationships, So much so that they allow themselves to be treated terribly. I recall a male friend sharing with me that his girlfriend kept telling him he did not love her because he had never hit her. "What a disgusting premise," I thought. How low of a self-esteem must one have to succumb to such nonsense? Eventually, he ended up hitting her.

I learned then that this was the way some women wanted

love to be expressed to them. This was new to me because my boyfriends were all Christians. I vowed that I would never let such foolishness happen to me. I even warned my husband before we were married to never have a lapse in judgment and try to hit me – since I was marrying into a whole different culture, I wanted to make sure my position was clear.

There were other instances (two, to be exact) where I observed the dead bodies of women who could not let go of abusive relationships because of the fear of being alone. In one case, a group of us were walking home from church one evening when we saw a commotion up ahead.

We inquired about what was happening and were told, "A man just chopped up his wife." We ran into the yard and then the house. There was the woman with cuts all over her body; she was dead. The neighbors kept saying, "We told her to leave him, but she would not listen." Fear of letting go led this woman to a horrible and painful death.

Yes, we belong to the animal kingdom, but we are not animals. We are part of a higher order that is commissioned to protect each other. If you know the Lord, then there are directives in scripture that we must follow. The story Jesus told of the Good Samaritan relates how the Samaritan's decision to help a stranger who was beaten, stripped of all his clothing and left for dead, made all the difference.

"….Jesus said: 'A man was going down from Jerusalem to Jericho, when he was attacked by robbers. They stripped him of his clothes, beat him and went away, leaving him half dead. A priest happened to be going down the same road, and when he saw the man, he passed by on the other side. So too a Levite, when he came to the place and saw him, passed by on the other side.

But a Samaritan, as he traveled, came where the man was; and when he saw him, he took pity on him. He went to him and bandaged his wounds, pouring on oil and wine. Then he put the man on his own donkey, brought him to an inn and took care of him. The next day he took out two denarii and gave them to the innkeeper. "Look after him," he said, "and when I return, I will reimburse you for any extra expense you may have."

Which of these three do you think was a neighbor to the man who fell into the hands of robbers?' The expert in the law replied, 'The one who had mercy on him.' Jesus told him, 'Go and do likewise.'" Luke 10:30-37 (NIV)

The Samaritan simply showed mercy. When we are hurting, mercy can be the furthest thing from our minds. Nevertheless, it is incumbent upon us as mere human beings to show mercy to each other. We need to be conscious that letting go does not only deal with relationships; it also addresses the hurts we carry deep inside.

Some of us carry hurts that even the person closest to us could be unaware of, hurts that can hinder a relationship because they are viewed through the eyes (lens) of past experiences. We all say we have forgiven at one time or another, but the next time that individual does something, we spew out the hurt from the past experience.

There are Bible stories that show that it is possible to

forgive when the choice is made to let go and do it. Read the story of Joseph (Genesis 37-50), Peter's denial of Jesus (Matthew 26:26-69), and the woman caught in adultery (John 8:1-11). We can all learn from these examples.

Over the years, I've seen many things done in the name of the Lord that could be considered abuse. Some leaders abused their positions by usurping their authority and punishing those who dared to disagree or who had a different opinion about something. I shared already that I know what it's like to be made to "sit down" and be inactive for a period of time only because I dared to disagree or shared an opinion.

I saw leaders use the pulpit to batter the church into submission. I was privy to believers' spirits being crushed and others hurting, but still they stayed. I often wondered why people subjected themselves to such abuse. I realized that many stayed because there were no other options.

Yet even in these circumstances, God still moved and people were still being blessed. What most people fail to realize is that God honors His word because He is committed to it; however, the vessel He uses might not always be His first choice (Balaam & the donkey Numbers 22:21-39).

I had built such a strong exterior that it was impossible to penetrate. At times I felt as if I were void of emotions. I would look at the way certain things affected others and wonder what the fuss was about. At one point, it seemed as if empathy was completely missing from my life. I would sit and ask myself why I was not affected about situations like others.

I had to make a concentrated effort to work on letting go of hurts and built-up resentments. What I was exposed to seemed to have affected me more than the individuals who were involved, because after a while, they went on their merry ways. Folks share things with you and you help them, but then they take you for granted. You appear to be the one left "holding the bag" while they go on about business as usual until something else happens again.

I would wear these "nothing is bothering me" looks, while deep inside, I was in pain. I was a total hypocrite! These experiences taught me that I was responsible for me. I had to recognize what I was dealing with and ask God for help.

> *"So then, each of us will give an account of ourselves to God." Romans 14:12 (NIV)*

This was done by taking an introspective look at my life and deciding that the buck stopped with me. I was the one who had to embody the change, whatever it might be. I had to be truthful and unmask anything and everything I was hiding behind. Hallelujah! Who the Son sets free is free indeed!

Unmasking The Walls

Built-up walls are the most dangerous things in any relationship. It is imperative, therefore, that they be identified in order to create and foster healthy and loving relationships. As children, we were trusting and open to others without reservations, depending on others to lead us. As we grow older, we learn that things do not always go our way, and to counteract that, we build walls. Walls can be used to cause division or imprisonment, depending on whether we are using them for our own security. Whether we recognize it or not, we build walls to block out the negative feelings and our reactions.

Mankind has this innate need for self-preservation, and in order to protect ourselves, we sometimes unknowingly build walls as a protective mechanism. What I have found is that instead of being a protection, the walls can hinder the fostering of true and meaningful relationships. There were times when I did not allow people to get too close because I was not sure of their agendas. I had (and sometimes still have) the tendency to psychoanalyze people. The walls I had built were carefully constructed to conceal any shortcoming I might have. This was done in the event that others saw something different from what they expected, since it could be attributed to someone else's capabilities or lack thereof.

I was always smart, witty, and the leader of the group, so it was sometimes difficult to determine if some friendships were truly for me or what association with me would offer. Don't get me wrong, I was no angel; some parts of me could get those around me into real trouble. I had the ability to take the meekest of persons and turn them into a rebel.

One example was a friend of mine, Jennifer, who was well behaved but wanted to hang out with my group. She got into so much trouble with us, but she was really a misfit because she was operating outside of her character. In retrospect, I can see how we took advantage of her because she was easily influenced.

The scriptures tell us:

> *"But encourage one another day after day, as long as it is still called 'Today,' so that none of you will be hardened by the deceitfulness of sin." Hebrews 3:13 (NASB)*

> *"Do not let any unwholesome talk come out of your mouths, but only what is helpful for building others up according to their needs, that it may benefit those who listen." Ephesians 4:29 (NIV)*

The walls I had built were not readily identifiable, but I knew they were there. Not only was being allowed to enter my sphere a challenge to those who wanted to be my friends, but it also required me to maintain this tough facade. I believe in my case it backfired, because I became really tough and unsympathetic. There was that tendency to display a tough exterior to impress others, but I used it to protect myself. It seemed as if I always had to navigate between who I was going to let in or even get close to. I don't know about you, but that was definitely no way to live.

Can you identify times when you retreated into your self-made cocoon and put up that wall, because you felt you were safer there? Or you physically ran into a room because you had a flashback of impending danger, whether it was real or not? I had to unmask my walls, but in order to do, so it was imperative that I become vulnerable. This took me out of my comfort zone. It was no longer about being safe but about trusting in the Lord to bring me out.

"The Lord is my helper; I will not be afraid. What can mere mortals do to me?" Hebrews 13:6 (NIV)

"The Lord will fight for you; you need only to be still." Exodus 14:14 (NIV)

"Keep me safe, my God, for in you I take refuge." Psalm 16:1 (NIV)

My walls were broken down as I surrendered completely to the Lord. How liberating that was; I was finally free from years of being tough and trying not to be vulnerable. Undoubtedly, vulnerability leaves you with a feeling of incompetence? Nevertheless, we must bare ourselves between and before our God and man. There is no need for fear, only the ability to trust in our God to work it all out, because our security lies in Him. Exposure – the very word conjures up fear, but we can be like King Hezekiah and turn to our Source.

"Hezekiah turned his face to the wall and prayed to the Lord." Isaiah 38:2 (NIV)

"Be strong and courageous. Do not be afraid or terrified because of them, for the Lord your God goes with you; he will never leave you nor forsake you." Deuteronomy 31:6 (NIV)

"Even to your old age and gray hairs I am he, I am he who will sustain you. I have made you and I will carry you; I will sustain you and I will rescue you." Isaiah 46:4 (NIV)

Along this journey, I soon recognized that if I wanted to

grow and move forward in God, I now had to meet with those I felt had hurt me by their actions and ask their forgiveness for my resentment. Surprisingly, once I made up my mind to do it, it was not as difficult as I thought. Not that I really wanted to do it, I definitely did not want to. However, I knew that the Word of God commands that we forgive others and allow the grace of God that is within us to be extended to them.

I by no means want to trivialize the hurt and pain you might have experienced. But living with hurt, bitterness, resentment, and unwillingness to forgive can ultimately destroy you. We must realize that forgiveness is as much for our own spiritual growth as it is for those who have hurt us. Therefore, I plead with you to forgive. Perhaps you have tried in your own strength and failed, but your heavenly Father is right there by your side to assist you.

> *"For if you forgive other people when they sin against you, your heavenly Father will also forgive you. But if you do not forgive others their sins, your Father will not forgive your sins."*
> *Matthew 6:14-15 (NIV)*

> *"Bear with each other and forgive one another if any of you has a grievance against someone. Forgive as the Lord forgave you." Colossians 3:13 (NIV)*

> *"Get rid of all bitterness and anger, brawling and slander, along with every form of malice. Be kind and compassionate to one another, forgiving each other, just as in Christ God forgave you." Ephesians 4:31-32 (NIV)*

"So, watch yourselves. If your brother or sister sins against you, rebuke them; and if they repent, forgive them. Even if they sin against you seven times in a day and seven times come back to you saying 'I repent,' you must forgive them." Luke 17:3-4 (NIV)

Year after year, and day by day as I grew in my Christian walk and relationship with my Father, I finally realized that God had me covered, and that He could protect me better than I could myself. His protection was sometimes in a still small voice, or a sense of peace and empowerment. Is protection something you still need? Reach out to Father God – "God is our refuge and strength, a very present help in trouble." Psalm 46:1 (ESV)

Remember, our God is stronger than the devil and anything the devil throws at us. Don't be like many and mistakenly put Jesus and the devil on equal plain, believing that they are opposites. How many times have you heard folks say "God is good and the devil is bad," as though they are opposites? This is an erroneous belief. God is the creator of the world and the whole universe, "and all that is in them," and the devil is a fallen angel who never created a single thing, neither does he have the ability to create. **They are not equal.** Scripture reads:

"Do you not know? Have you not heard? The Lord is the everlasting God, the Creator of the ends of the earth. He will not grow tired or weary, and his understanding no one can fathom." Isaiah 40:28 (NIV)

"And he swore by him who lives forever and

ever, who created the heavens and the earth and all that is in them, the earth and all that is in it..." Revelation 10:6 (NIV)

God, the Good Shepherd, will protect us; no one loves us more than He does. The Bible says He knows us by name; we are not lost in the sea of His creation. There is absolutely no limit to how far He will go to protect us. Let us unmask our walls and tear them down.

> *"Even though I walk through the darkest valley, I will fear no evil, for you are with me; your rod and your staff, they comfort me." Psalm 23:4 (NIV)*

> *"Be strong and courageous. Do not be afraid or terrified because of them, for the Lord our God goes with you; he will never leave you nor forsake you." Deuteronomy 31:6 (NIV)*

> *"But God is faithful, and he will strengthen you and protect you from the evil one." 2 Thessalonians 3:3 (NIV)*

Amen! And after we have done that, let's stop finding reasons for doing the things we did. There is really no reason to look back – remember Lot's wife (Genesis 19:12-29). Let us not be preoccupied with the things of the past, but let us stay focused on our future, stop justifying our actions, and simply relinquish control. The path the heavenly Father has charted and carved out for us is and will always be the right course.

> *"Whether you turn to the right or to the left, your ears will hear a voice behind you, saying,*

'This is the way; walk in it.'" Isaiah 30:21 (NIV)

Stop Justifying The Actions

"Therefore, confess your sins to each other and pray for each other so that you may be healed. The prayer of a righteous person is powerful and effective." James 5:16 (NIV)

In order to move forward and change, we must engage in behaviors that are becoming of a Christian. If we want to be a changed individual, we have to stop justifying why we did the things we did. Then, we must consciously make the effort to disregard all justifiable reasons we have in our minds. Almost all of us can debate why we are the way we are. Some would say it is because of heredity or culture, while those who are Christians might say it is in the blood line or a generational curse.

With this in mind, many find it easy to always have a reason as to why they are acting despicable. Disgusting behavior is never, ever inevitable. We all have a choice; we have the wherewithal to decide our course of actions. We can all change – change from the destructive road we are on to becoming the individual God intends us to be.

"I can do all things through Christ which strengthens me." Philippians 4:13 (KJV)

"Or do you not know that your body is a temple of the Holy Spirit within you, whom you have from God? You are not your own." 1 Corinthians 6:19 (ESV)

Like most of you, I found many reasons to justify my unwanted behavior. Life threw me a few curve balls, but how they were hit was entirely my decision. I could be like the baseball player who found every excuse to explain why he was striking out every time he came up to bat, until he realized that getting better at bat was up to him. Like that batter, I had to stop justifying my actions and behavior. I came to a point where I decided to let God be in control of my life. I put aside all negativity and surrendered to Christ. The Bible puts it this way: *"...lay aside every weight, and the sin which doth so easily beset us" (Hebrews 12:1, KJV)*. No more trying to be the defender of my life. In case you did not notice, that is a tiring way to live. The Word of God has a way of "coming alive" and addressing our situations as we read it.

> *"The law of the Lord is perfect, refreshing the soul. The statutes of the Lord are trustworthy, making wise the simple. The precepts of the Lord are right, giving joy to the heart. The commands of the Lord are radiant, giving light to the eyes. The fear of the Lord is pure, enduring forever. The decrees of the Lord are firm, and all of them are righteous. They are more precious than gold, than much pure gold; they are sweeter than honey, than honey from the honeycomb. By them your servant is warned; in keeping them there is great reward." Psalm 19:7-11 (NIV)*

Oh! How rewarding and fulfilling is a life dependent on the Lord! It is like fresh dew. As we walk with Him and commit ourselves to Him, we come in alignment with Him and His purposes for our lives. The Lord invites us to call upon Him, and He will show us the majestic things He has in store for us.

"Call to me and I will answer you and tell you great and unsearchable things you do not know." Jeremiah 33:3 (NIV)

He invites us to come walk with Him.

"Keep steady my steps according to your promise, and let no iniquity get dominion over me." Psalm 119:133 (ESV)

"He has told you, O man, what is good; and what does the Lord require of you but to do justice, and to love kindness, and to walk humbly with your God?" Micah 6:8 (ESV)

Chapter 6

Walking With the Lord

Enjoy The Comforts His Blessings Bring

"Commit to the Lord whatever you do, and he will establish your plans." Proverbs 16:3 (NIV)

"But blessed is the one who trusts in the Lord, whose confidence is in him. They will be like a tree planted by the water that sends out its roots by the stream. It does not fear when heat comes; its leaves are always green. It has no worries in a year of drought and never fails to bear fruit." Jeremiah 17:7-8 (NIV)

"Blessings" comes from the Hebrew word Barak, which means to give or receive an inheritance. I have received so many of God's blessings that it never ceases to amaze me. I know that my heavenly Father really does love me unconditionally. He finds all kinds of ways to show me His love. It could be from the littlest thing to something with more grandeur; still, I can see His hands entwined through them all.

"And we know that in all things God works for the good of those who love him, who have been

called according to his purpose." Romans 8:28
(NIV)

It was in July of 2003, that my family migrated to the United States. We are from Aruba as stated before. However, when my oldest daughter completed High School she asked if she could go to the USA instead of going to the Netherlands to further her studies. So, the decision was made that we would make the change as a family.

After being in the United States for 5 months I got my real estate license. Then in January of 2004, I entered college. I had not been in a secular school for over 30 years, but my girls were starting college, so I decided to join them. The first couple of weeks, I thought, "What have I gotten myself into?"

As a matter of fact, I cried in my math class as I looked at what the professor was writing on the board. I did not remember ever seeing those symbols when I completed high school back in 1973. The professor tried consoling me, and the students kept telling me it would be okay. In the end, it was okay; the students would say, "If Ms. Ingrid doesn't know it, then no one does."

I got an A in that math class, then took statistics (seems I liked punishment) and got an A there too. I excelled and took honors classes, then became the Vice President of the Phi Theta Kappa honor society and a member of the Beta Kappa Gamma honor society, both collegiate and national.

I practiced real estate until 2008, when I put my license

into the inactive status because I enrolled at Georgia State University. It may seem strange, but at university, it seemed as if I was in my element. It was a great adventure, as I went to university on a "free ride." In fact, I was paid to go to school, as I received various scholarships.

"Commit to the Lord whatever you do, and he will establish your plans." Proverbs 16:3 (NIV)

"But blessed is the one who trusts in the Lord, whose confidence is in him." Jeremiah 17:7 (NIV)

"May he give you the desire of your heart and make all your plans succeed." Psalm 20:4 (NIV)

While at Georgia State University, I became involved in areas that had nothing to do with my major. My degree was in Managerial Sciences, yet I became a McNair scholar. The McNair program is designed for STEM (science, technology, engineering, and mathematics) students, to prepare them for their doctorate degree. Yet I got into the program! "How was that possible?" you might ask, and my answer would be, "All because of the grace and favor of my Lord." I was the Vice President of the GHLA (Georgia Hotel & Lodging Association), GSU Hospitality Chapter. Again, my major was not even in Hospitality. But God! I was also a member of the Tau Sigma National Honor Society.

My involvement in these chapters afforded me some fantastic opportunities. As a McNair scholar, I had the privilege of spending a month attending the University of Salamanca in Salamanca, Spain. Then I was able to visit six countries in Europe through the Hospitality Department's study abroad program. These were invaluable opportunities and experiences that I could never have envisioned in my wildest dreams. There is nothing in this life, if we walk upright, that we could ever want that the Father is not willing to give us. He said:

> *"You may ask me for anything in my name, and I will do it." John 14:14 (NIV)*

After This What?

You have traveled with me on this journey, and perhaps you are wondering, "What has been the outcome of it all?". You are probably asking, "What has she learned throughout all this, and what does her life look like now?" I am happy to report that my life has come around full circle. From where I started to where I am now can only be attributed to the grace and mercies of God coupled with His loving kindness.

I am an ordained Apostle, and I am no longer that individual who struggled through the vicissitudes of life. I am amazed at the goodness of God. Oh! What God can do with a life that is dedicated and committed to Him! Today I stand as an entirely different individual in terms of my level of growth and the commission God has placed on my life. I am today truly that new creation in Christ. *I've got this, and I have come out of the "rain" – and, beloved, so can you.*

> *"So, from now on we regard no one from a worldly point of view. Though we once regarded Christ in this way, we do so no longer. Therefore,*

if anyone is in Christ, he is a new creation; the old has gone, the new has come!" 2 Corinthians 5:16-17 (NIV)

Interestingly, I was at a gathering not too long ago where I saw some of my old acquaintances. One indicated that she had a word from the Lord for me. As I stood there listening to the word, I had no identification with what was being said. Those words were for the old me, a person who was crucified many years ago (she had not seen me in over 20 years). I now walk in a totally different position and mantle. I am so happy with where I am, and who I am, in my relationship with my heavenly Father and the godly and anointed men and women with whom I am in covenant.

The power of knowing who you are in Christ is self-empowering. Recognizing the access, you have to a power that is greater than any other is chest-pumping and high-fiving. It is important to know who are in God for yourself. Do not allow others to define you, and neither should you constantly seek man's validation. Some folks find it necessary to flaunt positions and titles, and if you do not operate that way, they take no time to discern where you are spiritually. Therefore, they have no idea which of God's anointed you are and resort to thinking of the old you.

I know unequivocally who I am in God. I do not have a mere external form of religion, or pretending before men to be what I am not. I walk in the light of God's glorious gospel and possess the power of God.

The Bible says:

> *"He has shown you, O mortal, what is good. And what does the Lord require of you? To act justly and to love mercy and to walk humbly with your God."* Micah 6:8 (NIV)

> *"They may pretend to have a respect for God, but in reality, they want nothing to do with God's power. Stay away from people like these!"* 2 Timothy 3:5 (TPT)

After all this, what indeed! My eyes are set like flint as I continue in my Christian walk, calling, and commission. Christ controls my every being, and how glorious that is. I am beside myself with the vessel He is still making me into.

> *"For we are his workmanship, created in Christ Jesus for good works, which God prepared beforehand, that we should walk in them."* Ephesians 2:10 (ESV)

Forget those who I call Christian grave-diggers, whose only life purpose seems to be walking around digging up people's past for conversation. It always burns my heart when a new believer can recite another person's fall from grace that happened years ago, but that person had repented and moved on.

Know that after you have had a conversation with your heavenly Father and He has forgiven you, stand and walk comfortably in that. Now, if and when you are asked, "After this, what?" declare with all confidence, "God's got my back, for He has the final say."

God's Got the Final Say

Hallelujah! My destiny is in the hands of God. Going forward, I am forever grateful to my heavenly Father because He has the final say. He told me to **"come out of the rain."** I have relinquished control; I am overjoyed that my future is destined by God. There are so many promises He has made to me that I relish in them. Look at me now – my God has refined me, polished me, and now I look like fine gold. Some take my confidence for arrogance, but they have no idea of my life's journey.

I am so excited for the goodness of the Lord. He has brought me a mighty long way, as the old church mothers used to say. He has placed His stamp of approval on my life. I am living my best life. I am a child of the Living God, with a heavenly Father holding me close to His bosom. I love to speak of Him being the big-breasted one. His goodness is from everlasting to everlasting. He never withholds anything that is good from us, His children.

I have a family that means the world to me, a husband and children who spoil me. I want for nothing. The goodness of the Lord indeed overtakes me. He has placed people in my life who are dear to my heart. I came out on the other side because I depended on and trusted in the Lord. I did not allow bitterness to consume me. I am so glad that there was one constant in the way I lived. I was never able to bear malice – don't be fooled, I could be confrontational, but after it was over, I held no ill will.

No one can ever predict what a life committed to Jesus can look like, but just look at my life and you will definitely get an idea. The God whom I serve is real, just like the air you breathe. Never be afraid to walk in your conviction. Someone once said, "the past is a portion of your future lived;" also "It is not what you are that holds you back; it is what you think you are not." Remember, there is only one you, and you are unique. The things we hear and see concerning our lives are minuscule when compared to our own thought processes of how we perceive ourselves.

> *"Give thanks to the Lord, for he is good; his love endures forever. Let the redeemed of the Lord tell their story...." Psalm 107:1-2 (NIV)*

One of my favorite verses in the Bible is written by the great apostle Paul

> *"Being confident of this very thing, that he which hath begun a good work in you will perfect it until the day of Jesus Christ." Philippians 1:6 (KJV)*

A Closing Prayer

To close out this narrative, I thought I would leave this prayer with you. As you say this prayer, I want it to be purposeful, meaningful, and the cry of your heart. Do not just pray it as a collection of words, but allow it to resonate in your spirit. Prayer can be the foundation for us crying out to God when we are feeling the pressures that life brings.

"Dear heavenly Father, I thank you for the privilege of coming to you in prayer. Thank you that you are the true and living God. Thank you for being a caring, loving, and wonderful Father. Thank you that I can come before you just as I am, with my imperfections, baggages, hurts, disillusions, and brokenness. Thank you that I am privileged to come to you without fear of being rejected. Lord, I call out like Solomon, thank you for promising to hear and answer my prayers. Oh Lord, God of Israel, there is no God like you in all of heaven and earth. You keep your promises to a thousand generations and show unfailing love to all who walk before you in wholehearted devotion. Like Jeremiah, Lord, I realize that my life is not my own because I am not able to plan my own course. So, correct me, oh Lord, but be gentle; do not correct me in anger, for I would die. I need your help in walking on the course you have charted out for my life. My dependency is on you, dear Father, not on my own strength or abilities. I need you as that present constant in my life, oh Lord, for I can do nothing without you. I declare today that my life moving forward would be committed to you and my faith would be in you. I activate the power of God to be operative in my life. I will no longer allow the storms of life to shift my focus, but I will trust in you, Lord, to have an expected end. In Jesus' name I pray, Amen!"

Appendix

Abbreviated Bible Translations

AMP   Amplified Bible

CEBA   Common English Bible w/Apocrypha

ESV   English Standard Version

GNT   Good News Translation

KJV   King James Version

NASB   New America Standard Bible

NIV   New International Version

NLT   New Living Translation

www.ingramcontent.com/pod-product-compliance
Lightning Source LLC
Chambersburg PA
CBHW020921090426
42736CB00008B/735